Sewing Pretty Bags

Sewing Pretty Bags

Boutique Designs to Stitch & Love

Debra Valencia

Cheyanne Valencia

Design Originals

an Imprint of Fox Chapel Publishing

www.d-originals.com

To my mother, for purchasing my first sewing machine when I was
thirteen years old and purchasing fabric for everything I wanted to
make. And to my paternal grandmother, Socorro del Rosario Valencia,
for inspiring me during my teenage years to be creative, follow my
dreams, and see the world.
—Debra

To those who have kept an eye out for me and those who have always
believed in me.
I wouldn't trade you for the world.
Thanks for checking in.
—Cheyanne

Text by Debra Valencia,
Project design and step-by step photography by Cheyanne Valencia.

ACQUISITION EDITOR:
Peg Couch

COPY EDITORS:
Madison Glassmyer and
Laura Taylor

**COVER AND PAGE
DESIGNER:**
Ashley Millhouse

EDITOR:
Katie Weeber

**EDITORIAL
ADMINISTRATOR:**
Melissa Younger

LAYOUT DESIGNER:
Maura J. Zimmer

PROJECT PHOTOGRAPHY:
Scott Kriner

ISBN 978-1-57421-951-7

Library of Congress Cataloging-in-Publication Data

Valencia, Debra.
  Sewing pretty bags / Debra Valencia, Cheyanne Valencia.
    pages cm
  Includes index.
  ISBN 978-1-57421-951-7
  1. Handbags. 2. Sewing. I. Valencia, Cheyanne. II. Title.
  TT667.V35 2015
  646.4'8--dc23
                    2014041470

© 2015 by Debra Valencia, Cheyanne Valencia, and New Design Originals Corporation,
www.d-originals.com, an imprint of Fox Chapel Publishing,
800-457-9112, 1970 Broad Street, East Petersburg, PA 17520.

Printed in China
First printing

Contents

Retro Ruffles Purse 18

Summer Style Quilted Tote....26

Boho Girl Sling Bag 34

Peonies & Pearls
Messenger Bag................40

Cheyanne Valencia

Debra Valencia

About the Authors

Debra and Cheyanne come from a long line of creative women—you might say sewing is in their blood. Their maternal great-grandmother and paternal grandmother were both skilled sewers who used their talents to make clothes, quilts, and other fabric items for their families. Debra received her first sewing machine at the age of thirteen and was soon designing sewing patterns for herself, making her own clothes and room décor. Cheyanne blossomed as a seamstress later as an adult, launching her own business that features her handmade needle art crafts. In 2011, the sisters started working together, with Cheyanne designing and sewing fashionable projects to showcase the fabrics from Debra's successful fabric lines. This book is a culmination of their work together, featuring twelve of the projects they designed and created.

Debra Valencia is a visionary artist, designer, and entrepreneur with a passion for world travel, artisan traditions, and popular genres. Her designs take a fresh approach to creatively blending florals, paisleys, geometric, and decorative motifs, appealing to women who love bold color, fashion, and femininity. Debra is currently licensed with more than thirty product manufacturers in the gift, stationery, textiles, home décor, fashion accessories, bath/body, and cosmetics industries. Her designs have sold as quilting fabric collections for Blank Quilting Corporation, David Textiles, South Sea Imports, Wilmington Prints, and Spoonflower. Debra graduated with honors with a BFA from the University of Arts in Philadelphia. Sharing her knowledge with others is very important to Debra. She teaches art/design studio courses and art-related business courses at major colleges and universities, as well as seminars for creative professional organizations. Join her mailing list for sewing tips, patterns, freebies, and fabric source information at *debravalencia.com*.

Cheyanne Valencia is the sewing project designer and co-author of this book. Owner of Prairie Pony Mercantile in Montana, Cheyanne believes in doing things the old-fashioned way—by hand. She is carrying on the traditions of sewing and needle arts, creating hand-stitched, one-of-a-kind crafts to sell at local farmers' markets, craft fairs, quilt shows, festivals, and online. Learn more at *prairiepony.com*.

PHOTOGRAPHY BY MICHAEL LOHR PHOTOGRAPHY.

PHOTOGRAPHY BY JESSICA CHAVEZ.
We've loved working together and have had the opportunity to create some amazing projects. See page 34 for a variation of the Boho Girl Sling Bag shown above and page 18 for a variation of the Retro Ruffles Purse shown above right.

Introduction

Inside this book, you'll find twelve designs that we've created in collaboration. They are fresh, modern, and just a little sassy, but come together in a snap. We hope you are inspired to pull out the sewing machine and get creative! These pieces don't require a lot of fabric, so use them to clean out that fabric stash or to play with different combinations of pattern, color, and texture. If fabric selection seems daunting, try using fabric collections or precut bundles of coordinating fabrics to take the guesswork out of the process. Look for some tips on page 14 to start selecting your color palette and fabrics.

The simple construction of these pieces ensures fabulous results every time, with straight seams and minimal patterns. With detailed step-by-step instructions and photos, you will be guided through every step of the process. There are no specialized techniques or complicated procedures, so once you have your sewing machine set up and your fabric selected, you are ready to dive in! If you'd like a little guidance before you start, check out pages 12–13 for loads of helpful hints and tricks for success in the sewing room.

Each project has been set up to be super simple to use. At the beginning of each one, you will see a Materials & Tools list and a Cutting Chart. Use the Materials & Tools list as the shopping list for your project—it will tell you the amount of fabric you need to buy off the bolt in the store, as well as any additional supplies you might need. Then, once you have your fabric, follow the Cutting Chart to cut all the necessary pieces for the project. You will see the charts have been organized by fabric, so you can cut all the pieces from a particular fabric at once instead of going back and forth between fabrics!

These projects are made for you to stitch and love—whether you're looking for a sturdy grocery tote or a unique shoulder bag. So take the plunge and get sewing! We know you'll love the results!

— Debra & Cheyanne

PHOTOGRAPHY BY JESSICA CHAVEZ.
Shown here are some beautiful kitchen items Cheyanne created
using fabrics from Debra's Kyoto Hot Pink fabric collection.

Tips and Tricks

Cheyanne is the sewing project designer for this book and the maker of one-of-a-kind, hand-stitched crafts, so she is no stranger to the sewing room. Here are some of Cheyanne's top tips, tricks, and shortcuts to help you along your sewing journey.

Favorite tools

Disappearing marker. The disappearing marker is the handiest thing in the sewing room. It's an inexpensive tool that's easy to use, plus it's a *huge* time saver. Remember to follow the manufacturer's directions and test the marker on your fabric first to be sure it will disappear completely.

Rotary cutter. The rotary cutter is another great time saver. It might take a little time to get used to working with one, but once you get the hang of it, you'll never make a straight cut with scissors again! The blades are very sharp and last a long time. You can even cut through multiple layers of fabric with ease.

Cutting mat. A cutting mat is an essential tool to use with your rotary cutter. This special surface helps to keep your rotary blade sharp and protects your work surface from damage. Do not use a rotary cutter on any cardboard or wooden surface, as this will dull or damage the blade.

Clear quilting ruler. The clear quilting ruler is not just for quilters. These see-through rulers allow you to cut your measuring steps in half, while also making very precise angles for nice finished pieces. Use this ruler along with your disappearing marker and rotary cutter for all of your straight cut pieces.

Walking foot. A walking foot attachment for your sewing machine is a great investment if you do or are planning to do a fair amount of sewing. Once you sew with one, you won't know how you ever got along without it. I use mine in place of the regular A foot, even when it's not necessary, because it's such a pleasure to sew with. Visit your local craft, sewing, or quilting store to find a walking foot that fits your machine. If you're budget-conscious, wait for it to go on sale, as most stores selling sewing machines and accessories will have periodic sales on these items. You can also purchase this handy attachment online.

Favorite helpful hints

Prep your fabrics. Before starting any project, remember to wash and dry all new store-bought fabrics following the manufacturer's instructions to preshrink them and remove any sizing (light starch) that might have been applied. Press all the fabrics and true up the edges before cutting the necessary pieces.

Read ahead. Before starting any project, read through all the instructions to familiarize yourself with each step. Make sure you understand what needs to happen at each stage to ensure success.

Stay organized. Cut out all of the project pieces at once, unless directed otherwise. Keep them in groups with like pieces—pocket pieces, handle/strap pieces, lining pieces, body pieces, etc.—so they don't get mixed up. You can use your disappearing marker to label the pieces so you can recognize them at a glance.

Start small. Start by assembling the smallest pieces first, such as pockets and straps. Then work your way up to the larger lining and main body pieces. Always assemble the lining before the main body. This gives you a chance to work through any problem areas without anxiety, as any mistakes made will not be very visible in the finished piece. No one will know how many times you ripped out that seam and redid it as long as you are doing it with the lining pieces. And then you'll be fully prepared to assemble the main body of the project!

Press often. Keep your steam iron close to your workspace and press everything as you go. It's much nicer and easier to sew accurately on crisp, smooth fabric. Plus your finished piece will have a polished, professional look!

Favorite embellishment ideas

Embroidery. Hand embroidery is a classic way to embellish any sewing project and will make your finished piece truly unique. Embroidery floss comes in hundreds of colors to coordinate with your fabrics, and there are countless fun and easy stitches you can learn in a day or two. Draw your own design or mimic one of the motifs from your fabric like we've done on the Boho Girl Sling Bag (page 34).

Vintage collage. Vintage collage is another unique way to embellish a project. You can use vintage buttons, rhinestone pins or earrings, faux pearl necklaces, pieces of lace and ribbon, charms from an old charm bracelet, or even a vintage belt buckle. Sew these items onto your project by hand in a collage style to create a Victorian look or even a holiday theme. Turn vintage collage projects inside out before washing them, or use safety pins to pin a piece of soft fabric, such as t-shirt jersey, over the collage items to protect them during washing.

Monograms. Monogrammed items are popular and very stylish. If your project is intended as a gift, a monogram makes it extra special. Choose your favorite font and embroider your chosen letters, or cut the letters from a coordinating fabric and appliqué them onto the project like we've done with the Mod Monogram Backpack (page 46).

Fun trims. Trims, such as fringe, beaded fringe, pom-poms, and braided edging can be a fast and easy way to personalize your project. Many are sold by the yard, and you can create looks ranging from elegant to funky in a snap.

Pins. With just a little extra fabric, flower pins can be made to match any project, like the one we've made to match the Zen Yoga Bag (page 54). Follow the instructions on page 63 to make your own pin. You can make the pin in any size you'd like by using larger or smaller circle templates.

Fabric Selection

Are you ready to start your first pretty bag project? To begin, you'll need to select a nice array of fabrics that you love. Choosing fabric for a sewing project is really the most fun part (aside from wearing the end result!). You can play with pattern, design, and color. But all of those choices might seem a little overwhelming at first. Here are some tips and tricks you can use to choose the best fabrics every time.

Selection questions

Before you start the fabric selection process, consider these questions. Is the bag for you or a gift for someone else? Do you have a design theme or motif in mind (for example, feminine flowers or masculine geometrics)? If not, consider one now. Do you have a color scheme in mind? If not, think about your options now. What outfit do you want to pair the bag with? What's the overall style that you want—bold and modern or simple and traditional?

Fabric types

I recommend using 100% cotton fabric for the majority of your sewing projects (avoid any fabrics that have synthetic fibers, including blends). Cotton handles beautifully, doesn't stretch, is easy to cut, holds a crease well, and isn't slippery between your fingers. It will make the sewing process super easy, especially if you are a beginner.

If you're an experienced sewer or feeling adventurous, though, it's nice to try something out of the ordinary every now and then. Mix things up by experimenting with cozy flannel, glittery fabrics, faux fur, synthetic suede, or leather. Using these off the wall fabrics will create embellishments for you, such as a fur-lined pocket or a leather strap. Just remember, these fabrics might require a bit more effort or some special techniques, as they can be stretchy, stiff, or extra thick. But the extra effort is definitely worthwhile to create a totally unique project.

Color palette

With the thousands of color choices available, this task can seem a bit overwhelming. Just take it step by step—the more projects you make, the easier it will become. Here are some tips to help you choose your color palette.

To create a cohesive color palette, it is always helpful to consult the good old color wheel. Locate a color you like on the wheel and note which colors are next to it (analogous) and opposite it (complementary). You can use these related colors to build a harmonious palette as described below.

Feature fabric. Is there a fabric at the store that's already caught your eye? Why not build your color scheme around that fabric? I like to work with a palette where one fabric is dominant, and then I'll add up to three coordinating fabrics depending on the project. If you already have a fabric in mind and are looking to build around it, take a look at the selvages—there is often manufacturer information printed there, including swatches of the colors used in that specific fabric. You can use these swatches to identify the specific shade of each color utilized in the fabric. Carefully evaluate all of the different colors and narrow them down to the ones you want to use. From there, you can easily match other fabrics to the swatches and be confident that the colors coordinate. If you don't have a feature fabric in mind, see below for some other ideas for creating a color palette.

Neutral pairing. A failsafe approach to choosing a color scheme is to select one dominant color and pair it with a neutral, such as black, gray, tan, or ivory. This is a sure bet when you intentionally want your bag to match a particular outfit.

Monochromatic. A simple, clean color approach is to go monochromatic. This palette uses one color in varying shades and intensities, from light to dark (for example, shades of blue or pink). This is a great color scheme for gift projects, as you can make the project in shades of your recipient's favorite color.

Warm and cool. An easy way to choose a color scheme is to select all warm or all cool colors. Warm colors (red, orange, and yellow) will always look great together, as will cool colors (green, blue, and purple). I love designing my fabric collections with this type of palette. For example, I love using the warm palette of hot pink, light pink, orange, and yellow and the cool palette of blue and green.

Analogous. A warm or cool color scheme can also be called analogous. Analogous colors are adjacent to each other on the color wheel, so a warm color scheme might use the analogous colors red, orange, and yellow. But analogous color schemes aren't limited to only warm or only cool colors. For example, an analogous color scheme could mix the cool colors blue and green with the warm color yellow, or the cool color purple with the warm colors pink and red. If you select three or four adjacent colors from the color wheel, you will have a harmonious palette every time.

Complementary colors. Another direction is to select complementary colors. These are colors opposite one another on the color wheel, so this palette often mixes warm and cool colors. This type of color scheme can be too bold if you are using bright, highly saturated colors (like bright red and neon green, or neon orange and bright blue.) But using more muted, pastel shades can yield a very sophisticated look (like pale pink and light lime green).

By collection. When in doubt, choose fabrics from the same collection as created by textile designers like me and others featured in this book. Fabric manufacturers and designers do the work for you. Coordinated collections of fabric in different colors and print scales are intended to be used together, so you can be assured that everything will blend in harmony.

Just ask. If you still feel overwhelmed by all of the options, keep in mind that most fabric store personnel are experienced seamstresses. Their job is to assemble fabric collections that go well together for displays and sample projects. Be sure to tap into the suggestions of these pros when you drop by your local retailer for browsing or buying.

The Projects

It's time to get sewing! Whether you're looking for a practical bag with some simple adornments or an all-out statement piece, you're sure to find something you love here. Experiment with color, pattern, texture, and embellishment to make each piece fit your personal taste and style. And most important, have fun doing it!

How to Use This Book

We've tried to make the projects in this book simple and quick so you can have success every time and the instant gratification of making something fabulous in a few hours. At the beginning of each project, you will see a Materials & Tools list. Use this as your shopping list—it will tell you the amount of fabric you need to buy off the bolt in the store, as well as any additional supplies you might need. Once you have your fabric, follow the Cutting Chart to cut all the necessary pieces for your project. You will see the charts have been organized by fabric, so you can cut all the pieces from a particular fabric all at once. When your pieces are cut, you're ready to take them to the sewing machine and get going!

Retro Ruffles Purse

Materials & Tools:
- Fabric A: ½ yd. (0.5m) cotton or other (outer bag, handles)
- Fabric B: ½ yd. (0.5m) cotton or other (lining, pocket)
- Fabrics C & D: ¼ yd. (0.25m) each cotton or other (ruffles)
- Lightweight, fusible interfacing: 1 yd. (1m), 17" (43cm) wide
- Rickrack or trim of your choice: ¾ yd. (0.7m)

This ruffled purse is so feminine and fabulous, you'll want to keep it for yourself instead of giving it away as a gift! Coordinate the fabrics' colors and theme, or simply use random scraps to make an eclectic ensemble.

Cutting Chart

Follow the chart below to cut the pieces for this project from the total fabric yardage indicated in the Materials & Tools list above.

Piece Name	Material to Cut	Size to Cut	Quantity
Outer bag	Fabric A	13" x 13" (33 x 33cm)	2
Handle (cut on grain)	Fabric A	4" x 25½" (10 x 64.5cm)	2
Lining	Fabric B	13" x 13" (33 x 33cm)	2
Pocket	Fabric B	13" x 13" (33 x 33cm)	1
Ruffles	Fabrics C & D	4½" x 41" (11.5 x 104cm)	4 total (2 from each fabric)
Interfacing	Lightweight, fusible	12¾" x 12¾" (32.5 x 32.5cm)	2
Pocket interfacing	Lightweight, fusible	6" x 12¾" (15 x 32.5cm)	1

Tip

For economy, the ruffle fabric for this bag was cut selvage to selvage. While this is against the grain and wouldn't work well for apparel or projects where stretching is a concern, it works wonderfully for this petite handbag. With the selvages removed, your ruffle strips will be about 41" (104cm) long.

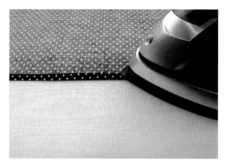

1 Prepare the pocket. Fold over the top and bottom edges of the pocket piece by ¼" (6mm). Press the folds in place. Fold the pocket in half, bringing the pressed edges together with wrong sides facing. Press the fold.

2 Apply the interfacing. Open the pocket and align the interfacing over one half of the pocket on the wrong side. Following the manufacturer's instructions, fuse the interfacing to the fabric.

3 Position the pocket. Fold the pocket in half once more. Using a disappearing marker, draw a vertical line down the center of the pocket from the top to bottom edges. Vertically center the pocket on top of the right side of one of the lining pieces. Position the pocket so that the half fold is at the top. Pin the pocket in place.

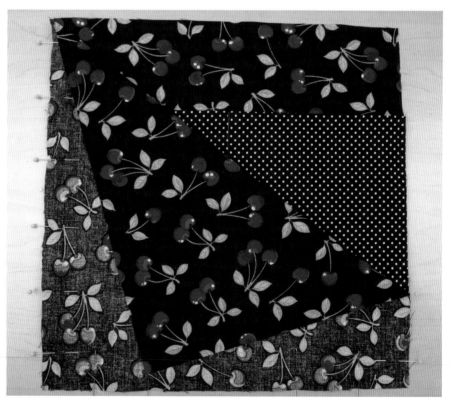

4 Stitch the pocket in place. Using a ⅛" (3mm) seam allowance, stitch along the bottom edge of the pocket to attach it to the lining piece. Then stitch along the centerline you drew on the pocket in Step 3. Stitch from the bottom of the pocket upward to prevent puckering. Finally, using a ¼" (6mm) seam allowance, baste the sides of the pocket to the lining piece.

5 Stitch the lining. Place the two lining pieces together with right sides facing and pin them in place. Using a ½" (1.5cm) seam allowance, sew along the side and bottom edges, leaving the top open. Leave a 6" (15cm) opening for turning along the center of the bottom edge. Remember to backstitch on both sides of the opening for turning. Trim the seam allowances with pinking shears.

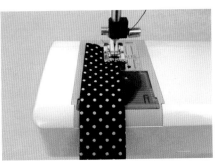

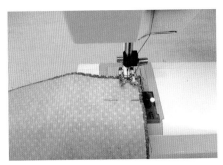

6 **Prepare the handles.** Fold each handle piece in half lengthwise with wrong sides facing and press the fold in place. Open each handle piece, and fold each long edge in until it meets the center crease. Press these folds in place.

7 **Stitch the handles.** Fold each handle in half lengthwise along the center crease as before. Stitch along the long open edge using a ⅛" (3mm) seam allowance. Leave the short ends raw.

8 **Stitch the outer bag.** Following the manufacturer's instructions, fuse a piece of interfacing to the wrong side of each of the outer bag pieces. Place the pieces together with right sides facing and pin them in place. Using a ½" (1.5cm) seam allowance, sew around the side and bottom edges, leaving the top open. Trim the seam allowances with pinking shears.

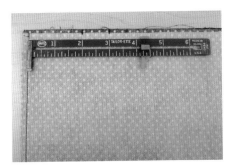

9 **Mark the handle placement.** On the wrong side of the outer bag fabric, measure in from each side seam and make a mark on the top edge at 2" (5cm) and 3" (7.5cm). Flip the outer bag over and repeat on the opposite side. This marks the placement for the handles.

10 **Mark the ruffle placement.** Turn the outer bag right side out. On the front of the bag, draw four lines parallel to the top and bottom edges at 3" (7.5cm), 5" (12.5cm), 7" (17.5cm), and 9" (22.5cm) from the bottom of the bag. Repeat on the back side. This marks the placement for the ruffles.

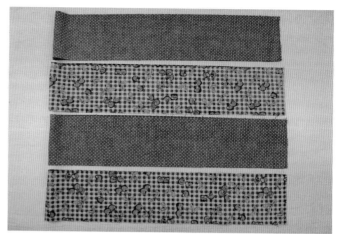

11 **Attach the trim.** Pin the rickrack or other trim of your choice around the outer bag, positioning it 1" (2.5cm) from the top edge. Sew straight down the center of the trim using a matching thread. Before stitching the finishing end of the trim in place, fold it under by ¼" (6mm) so it overlaps the starting end of the trim.

12 **Prepare the ruffles.** If you haven't done so already, trim the selvages from the ends of your ruffle strips. Fold each strip in half widthwise (bring the short ends together) with right sides facing. Stitch along the open short end of all the strips using a ¼" (6mm) seam allowance. This will form a loop. Trim the seam allowances of all the strips with pinking shears and press the seams open. Make sure all of the loops are about the same length so they will gather to about the same size.

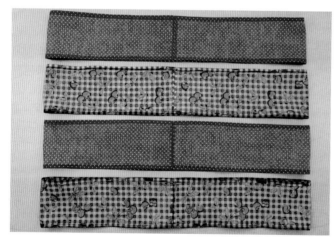

13 **Hem the ruffles.** Fold over the top and bottom edges of each ruffle loop by ¼" (6mm). Press these folds in place. Repeat, folding the edges over again and pressing them in place. Stitch the double folds in place using a ⅛"–⅜" (3–10mm) seam allowance.

14 **Mark the ends.** Lay each ruffle loop flat and place a pin in each short end to mark it. Leave these pins in place as you sew the gathering stitches.

 Tip

The project shown uses two different fabrics for the ruffles, but you could use four fabrics (one for each ruffle) if you wanted!

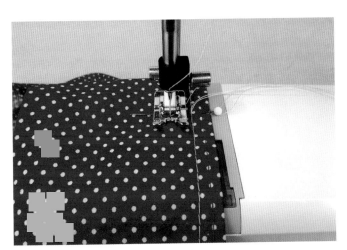

15 **Sew the gathering stitches.** Set the stitch length on your machine to 5. Sew two parallel rows of gathering stitches halfway around the top edge (from pin to pin) of one of the ruffle loops. The rows of stitches should be about ⅜" (1cm) and ¾" (2cm) from the edge. Make sure you leave long starting tails with both your machine and bobbin threads. Remove the ruffle from the machine and trim the ending threads, leaving long tails. If it's helpful, tie each set of machine and bobbin threads together with a slipknot so you can easily identify the pairs later. Rotate the ruffle and repeat, stitching the other half of the top edge from pin to pin. Repeat with all of the ruffle loops.

Tip

When sewing gathering stitches, use a contrasting color of thread for the bobbin thread. This way, you can easily tell the machine and bobbin threads apart.

16 **Place a ruffle.** Take a ruffle loop and attach the pins in the loop to each side of the outer bag. Align the top, stitched edge of the ruffle loop with the lowest horizontal line drawn on the outer bag.

17 **Gather a ruffle.** Secure the threads on the left side of the ruffle loop attached to the bag. Pull on the bobbin threads on the right side of the loop. This will begin to gather the fabric on one half of the loop. Continue pulling and gathering the ruffle until it is the same width as the bag (12" [30.5cm]). Then position the gathers evenly across the front of the bag and pin them in place. Flip the bag over and repeat to gather the ruffle fabric on the back side.

Tip

When gathering fabric, always pull on the bobbin threads instead of the machine threads. The bobbin threads are easier to pull and less likely to break than the machine threads.

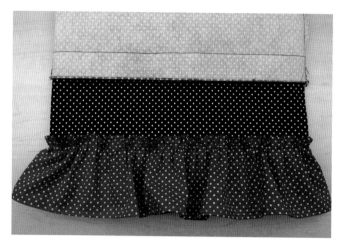

18 **Stitch a ruffle.** Fold the top of the outer bag down over itself so the bag will fit more easily onto your sewing machine. Sew the bottom ruffle in place by stitching ½" (1.5cm) from the top edge (between your rows of gathering stitches). Use a seam ripper to remove the gathering threads from the ruffle when finished.

19 **Attach the remaining ruffles.** Repeat Steps 16 –18 to attach the remaining ruffle loops to the outer bag.

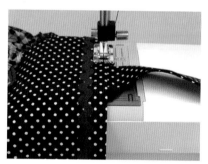

20 **Baste the handles.** Using the marks you made in Step 9, pin the handle ends to the outer bag, aligning the short ends of the handles with the top edge of the bag. Make sure the handles are not twisted. Baste the ends in place using a ¼" (6mm) seam allowance.

21 **Attach the lining.** Nest the outer bag inside the lining with right sides facing. Align the side seams and the raw top edges and pin the pieces in place. Stitch around the top edge of the bag using a ½" (1.5cm) seam allowance. Trim the seam allowance with pinking shears.

22 **Finish the bag.** Turn the bag right side out through the opening left in the bottom of the lining for turning. Hand stitch the opening closed using a blind stitch. Nest the lining inside the bag and press the top edge. Using a ⅛" (3mm) seam allowance, stitch around the top edge of the bag.

Summer Style Quilted Tote

Materials & Tools:

- Fabric A: ¼ yd. (0.25m) cotton or other (outer bag vertical band)
- Fabric B: ¾ yd. (0.7m) cotton or other (outer bag vertical band, lining, handles, button loop)
- Fabrics C & D: ¼ yd. (0.25m) each cotton or other (outer bag vertical bands)
- Fabric E: ⅓ yd. (0.3m) or fat quarter cotton or other (pocket)
- Cotton batting: 1 yd. (1m)
- Grosgrain or satin ribbon: 2 yd. (2m), 1½" (38mm) wide
- Button: 2" (50mm) diameter
- Walking foot

This quilted tote is extra sturdy due to its vertical strip construction, batting, and gusseted bottom. It is strong enough to hold books, your computer, and any other items that need to travel with you. The piece shown features a coordinated, Asian-inspired fabric collection with a coconut shell button. For a preppy look, try using fabrics with a small print in a monochromatic color scheme.

Cutting Chart

Follow the chart below to cut the pieces for this project from the total fabric yardage indicated in the Materials & Tools list above.

Piece Name	Material to Cut	Size to Cut	Quantity
Outer bag vertical band	Fabric A	5" x 17" (12.5 x 43cm)	2
Outer bag vertical band	Fabric B	5" x 17" (12.5 x 43cm)	2
Lining	Fabric B	17" x 17" (43 x 43cm)	2
Handles	Fabric B	4" x 21" (10 x 53.5cm)	2
Button loop	Fabric B	4" x 11" (10 x 28cm)	1
Outer bag vertical band	Fabric C	5" x 17" (12.5 x 43cm)	2
Outer bag vertical band	Fabric D	5" x 17" (12.5 x 43cm)	2
Pocket	Fabric E	12" x 12" (30.5 x 30.5cm)	1
Batting*	Cotton	19" x 19" (48.5 x 48.5cm)	2
Ribbon	Grosgrain or satin	1½" x 70" (38mm x 180cm)	1

Cut the batting in Step 11 after the front and back panels are made.

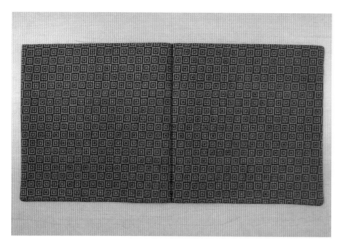

1 **Prepare the pocket.** Fold the pocket in half with right sides facing and pin it in place. Stitch around the open raw edges using a ½" (1.5cm) seam allowance. Leave a 3" (7.5cm) opening for turning along the center of the bottom long edge. Remember to backstitch on both sides of the opening for turning. Trim the seam allowances with pinking shears, and turn the pocket right side out. Using a disappearing marker, draw a vertical line down the center of the pocket from the top to bottom edges.

2 **Prepare the handles.** Fold each handle piece in half lengthwise with wrong sides facing and press the fold in place. Open each handle piece and fold each long edge in until it meets the center crease. Press these folds in place. Fold each handle in half lengthwise along the center crease as before. Stitch along the long open edge using a ⅛" (3mm) seam allowance. Leave the short ends raw.

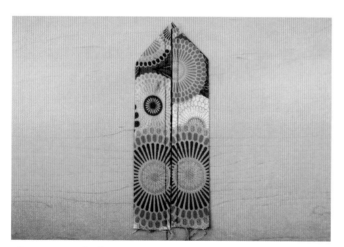

3 **Prepare the button loop.** Repeat Step 2 with the button loop piece to press and stitch the button loop. Then, fold each end of the strip down from the center point to create an arrow shape. Press the folds in place to hold the shape.

4 **Stitch the button loop.** Fold down the pointed tip of the button loop to form a rectangular shape as shown. Press the fold in place, and then stitch along the edges of the triangle shape using a ⅛" (3mm) seam allowance.

5 **Position the pocket.** Lay the pocket on top of the right side of one of the lining pieces, 3" (7.5cm) from the top edge and centered from side to side. Position the pocket so that the fold is at the top and pin it in place.

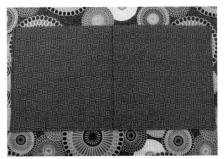

6 **Stitch the pocket in place.** Using a ⅛" (3mm) seam allowance, stitch around the sides and bottom edge of the pocket to attach it to the lining piece. Then stitch along the centerline you drew on the pocket in Step 1. Stitch from the bottom of the pocket upward to prevent puckering.

7 **Stitch the lining.** Place the two lining pieces together with right sides facing. Using a ½" (1.5cm) seam allowance, sew along the sides and bottom edge, leaving the top open. Leave a 6" (15cm) opening for turning along the center of the bottom edge. Remember to backstitch on both sides of the opening for turning. Use pinking shears to trim the seam allowances.

8 **Cut the corners.** Measuring from the seam line (not the edge of the fabric), draw 2" (5cm) squares in the bottom corners of the lining. Then cut out the squares.

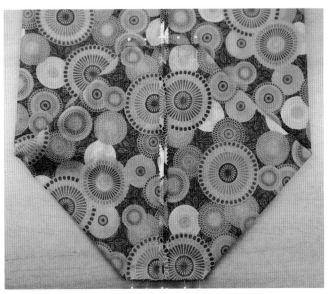

9 **Fold and stitch the corners.** Fold the lining fabric so the side seams align with the bottom seam and the bottom corners form straight raw edges as shown. Pin the corners in place, and then stitch straight along the raw edges using a ½" (1.5cm) seam allowance. Trim the seam allowances with pinking shears.

10 **Stitch the front and back panels.** Lay out one set of outer bag pieces in the order of A, B, C, and D with the long edges side by side. Stitch the four pieces together along the long edges using a ½" (1.5cm) seam allowance. Press all the seams open. Repeat with the remaining outer bag pieces to form the second panel.

11 **Quilt the front and back panels.** Lay each panel piece on top of the batting and trim the batting to ½" (1.5cm) larger than the panels on all sides. Use a disappearing marker to mark the desired quilting lines on each of the panels, and then pin each panel to its corresponding batting piece. Place a walking foot in your sewing machine and quilt each panel as desired.

 Tip

Use a walking foot to quilt the front and back panels. This foot has its own feed dogs on the bottom that help move your fabric and batting layers together as you stitch to avoid bunching and puckering.

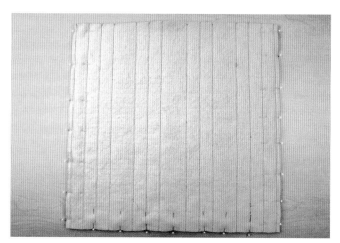

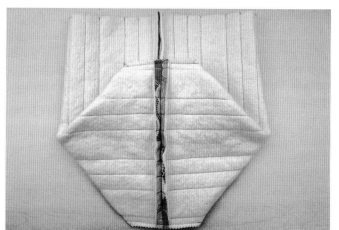

12 **Stitch the outer bag.** Trim away the excess batting from the edges of each panel piece. Place the panels together with right sides facing and pin them in place. Using a ½" (1.5cm) seam allowance, sew around the side and bottom edges, leaving the top open.

13 **Trim and stitch the corners.** Measuring from the seam line (not the edge of the fabric), draw 2" (5cm) squares in the bottom corners of the outer bag and cut them out as you did with the lining. Fold the outer bag so the side seams align with the bottom seam and the bottom corners form straight raw edges as shown. Pin the corners in place, and then stitch straight along the raw edges using a ½" (1.5cm) seam allowance. Trim the seam allowances with pinking shears.

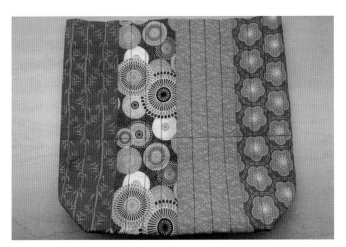

14 **Mark the ribbon placement.** Turn the outer bag right side out. Measure and draw a horizontal line across the front of the bag, parallel to the top and bottom edges, 8" (20.5cm) from the top edge. Repeat on the back side. This marks the placement of the ribbon embellishment.

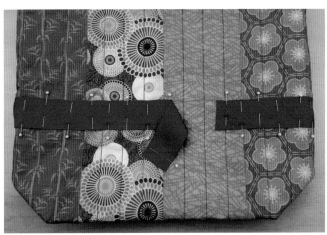

15 **Position the ribbon.** Cut a 33" (85cm)-long piece of ribbon. Place one end of the ribbon where you would like the bow to be located, aligning the top edge with the mark you made in Step 14. Wrap the ribbon around the body of the bag, working to the right and pinning both long edges in place. When you reach the opposite (left) end of the ribbon, leave about 3" (7.5cm) unpinned.

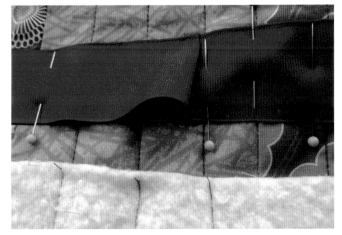

16 **Start sewing the ribbon.** Fold the top of the outer bag down over itself so the bag will fit more easily onto your sewing machine. Using a ¹⁄₁₆" (2mm) seam allowance, stitch the top edge of the ribbon in place. When you reach the end of the ribbon you left unpinned, fold it under by about ½" (1.5cm) so it overlaps the starting end of the ribbon and stitch it in place.

17 **Finish sewing the ribbon.** Repeat Step 16 to stitch the bottom edge of the ribbon in place. Move the unsewn folded end of the ribbon out of the way to start your stitching. When finished, press the ribbon with a steam iron to smooth out any wavy edges.

Tip

Leave the ribbon pins in place until both Steps 16 and 17 are complete to keep the ribbon from shifting.

18 **Prepare the bow.** Cut a 30" (76cm)-long piece of ribbon. Use a disappearing marker to draw marks at 8" (20.5cm), 16" (41cm), 22" (56cm), and 28" (67cm) from one end of the ribbon. Mark both the front and back of the ribbon.

19 **Fold the bow.** Starting with the end of the ribbon closest to the 8" (20.5cm) mark, fold the end over until it meets the 8" (20.5cm) mark. Then fold the other end of the ribbon over, matching up the 8" (20.5cm) and 16" (41cm) marks. Continue folding the ribbon over, aligning the marks until it looks like this.

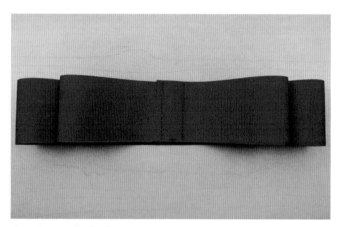

20 **Stitch the bow.** Pin the folds in place and stitch two lines across the width of the bow, about ¼" (6mm) on either side of the center point. Trim away any excess ribbon.

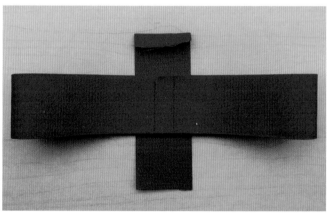

21 **Prepare the knot.** Cut a 4½" (11.5cm)-long piece of ribbon. Fold over one end by ½" (1.5cm) and press it in place. Lay the bow face down on top of the short knot piece, perpendicular to it so the pieces form a cross.

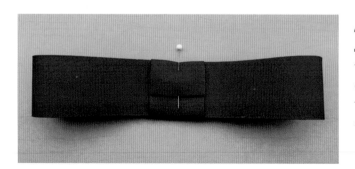

22 **Stitch the knot.** Fold over the raw end of the knot piece onto the bow. Then fold over the folded end of the knot piece onto the bow over top of the raw end. Pin the ends in place. Pin the bow onto the bag over the seam where the ends of the bag ribbon meet. Sew the bow in place by stitching close to the edges of the center knot ribbon.

23 **Baste the handles.** Pin the handle ends to the outer bag, aligning the short ends of the handles with the top edge of the bag. Align the sides of the handles with the left side of piece B and the right side of piece C. Baste the ends in place using a ¼" (6mm) seam allowance.

24 **Baste the button loop.** Pin the button loop onto the back side of the bag, centered along the top edge with the triangle shape face down. Align the short raw end of the button loop with the top edge of the bag. Baste the end in place using a ¼" (6mm) seam allowance.

25 **Sew the button.** Hand sew the button centered on the front of the bag. The center of the button should be about 2" (5cm) from the top edge. Fold the button loop over onto the front of the bag if necessary to help with button placement.

26 **Attach the lining.** Nest the outer bag inside the lining with right sides facing. Align the side seams and the raw top edges and pin the pieces in place. Stitch around the top edge of the bag using a ½" (1.5cm) seam allowance. Trim the seam allowance with pinking shears.

27 **Finish the bag.** Turn the bag right side out through the opening left in the bottom of the lining for turning. Hand stitch the opening closed using a blind stitch. Nest the lining inside the bag and press the top edge. Using a ⅛" (3mm) seam allowance, stitch around the top edge of the bag.

Boho Girl Sling Bag

Materials & Tools:

• Fabric A: 1 yd. (1m) cotton or other (outer bag, inside pocket, shoulder pad)
• Fabric B: ¼ yd. (0.25m) cotton or other (outer pocket)
• Fabric C: 1 yd. (1m) cotton or other (lining, shoulder pad lining)
• Batting (optional): 1 yd. (1m)
• Walking foot (if using batting)
• Embroidery floss (optional)

This boho bag, or sling bag, is the perfect casual accessory to pair with jeans, shorts, a skirt, or a long dress. It's super easy to sew, making it a perfect project for beginners. The project shown features color-coordinated fabrics, but you could also mix and match fabric scraps for a truly Bohemian look.

Before you begin

Use the diagram and instructions on page 124 to cut the outer bag and lining front and back pieces. To cut the pieces from a yard of fabric, fold the fabric twice to yield both pieces. All of the pocket pieces can be cut from the remnants.

Cutting Chart

Follow the chart below to cut the pieces for this project from the total fabric yardage indicated in the Materials & Tools list above.

Piece Name	Material to Cut	Size to Cut	Quantity
Outer bag (front/back; see page 124)	Fabric A	18" x 32" (45.5 x 81cm)	2
Inside pocket	Fabric A	8" x 6½" (20.5 x 16.5cm)	2
Shoulder pad	Fabric A	4¼" x 7" (11 x 18cm)	1
Outer pocket	Fabric B	5¼" x 8" (13.5 x 20.5cm)	4
Lining (front/back; see page 124)	Fabric C	18" x 32" (45.5 x 81cm)	2
Shoulder pad lining	Fabric C	4¼" x 7" (11 x 18cm)	1
Outer bag batting (optional)*		18" x 32" (45.5 x 81cm)	2
Shoulder pad batting (optional)*		4¼" x 6" (11 x 15cm)	1
Ribbon	Grosgrain or satin	1½" x 70" (38mm x 180cm)	1

If using batting, cut the fabric pieces from the paper pattern first. Then use a lining piece folded in half as your pattern to cut the batting. It's much easier to work with a fabric pattern on batting. Just be careful not to cut your lining piece.

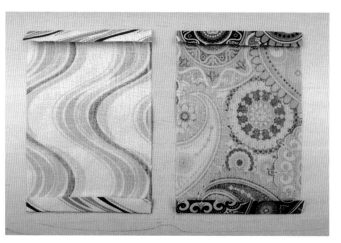

1 Prepare the pockets. Place the inside and outside pocket pieces together in pairs with right sides facing and pin them together (there are two outside pockets and one inside pocket). Using a ½" (1.5cm) seam allowance, sew around all the edges of each pocket pair, leaving a small opening for turning in one of the short sides. Remember to backstitch on both sides of the opening for turning. Clip the corners, trim the seam allowances, turn the pockets right side out, and press them. If desired, embroider a design on the front of one or both of the outside pockets.

2 Prepare the shoulder pad pieces. Fold over the short ends of both shoulder pad pieces by ½" (1.5cm) and press the folds in place.

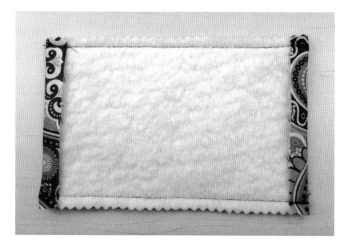

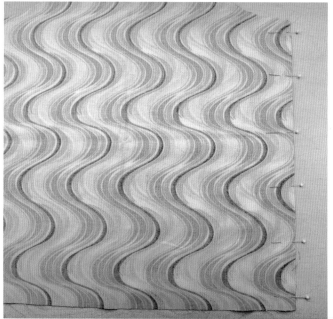

3 Attach the batting. Place the two shoulder pad pieces together with right sides facing. Then layer the batting on top, tucking the edges of the batting under the folded ends of the fabric. Pin everything in place and stitch along both long edges using a ½" (1.5cm) seam allowance. Leave the two short ends raw. Turn the shoulder pad right side out and press it.

4 Prepare the lining. Place the two lining pieces together with right sides facing. Pin the pieces together along one of the straight sides. Stitch along the pinned side using a ½" (1.5cm) seam allowance. Trim the seam allowance with pinking shears and press the seam open.

5 **Attach the inside pocket.** Place the lining piece right side up. The seam you just stitched in Step 4 should be in the center. Center the inside pocket over the seam, positioning the top long edge 2½" (6.5cm) from the top edge of the lining. Using a ⅛" (3mm) seam allowance, stitch around the side and bottom edges of the inside pocket. This will close the opening for turning you left in the pocket in Step 1.

6 **Sew the remaining side.** Fold the lining along the seam you made in Step 4 with right sides facing. Pin and stitch the open side using a ½" (1.5cm) seam allowance. Trim the seam allowance with pinking shears and press the seam open.

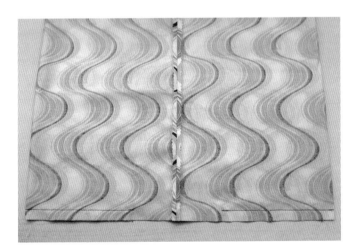

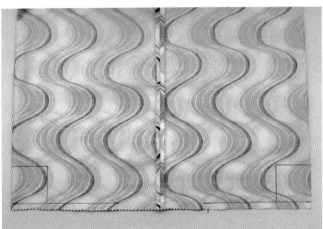

7 **Sew the bottom edge.** Refold the lining piece so the two seams are aligned and in the center as shown. Right sides are still facing. Using a ½" (1.5cm) seam allowance, stitch along the open bottom edge, leaving a 5"–6" (13–15cm) opening for turning. Remember to backstitch on both sides of the opening for turning. Trim the seam allowance with pinking shears.

8 **Mark the corners.** Measure and mark 2" (5cm) squares in the bottom corners of the lining. NOTE: When measuring the squares, do not include the bottom seam allowance; measure from the bottom stitch line instead of the bottom edge. Cut out the squares.

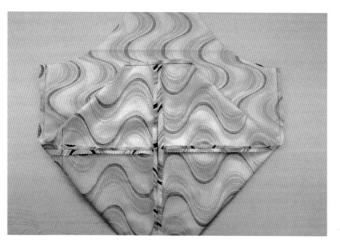

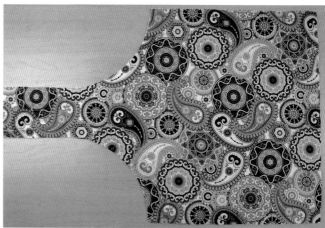

9 **Fold and stitch the corners.** Fold the lining fabric so the center seams and bottom seams form a cross over the bottom of the bag and the bottom corners form straight raw edges as shown. Pin the corners in place, and then stitch straight along the raw edges using a ½" (1.5cm) seam allowance. Trim the seam allowance.

10 **Baste the batting.** Layer an outer bag piece on top of each batting piece with the right side facing up. Press each outer bag piece on top of the batting. This eliminates any air pockets between the fabric and batting. Pin the pieces together. Using a ¼" (6mm) seam allowance, baste the batting to the outer bag pieces.

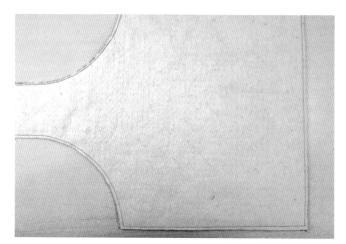

11 **Prepare the outer bag pieces.** Repeat Step 4 with the outer bag pieces, sewing them together along one straight side with right sides facing.

12 **Attach the outside pockets.** Place the outer bag right side up. The seam you just stitched in Step 11 should be in the center. Place the outside pockets on the outer bag piece, positioning the top short edges 2½" (6.5cm) from the top edge of the bag. Each pocket should be 2" (5cm) out from the center seam. Using a ⅛" (3mm) seam allowance, stitch around the side and bottom edges of the pockets. This will close the opening for turning you left in the pockets in Step 1.

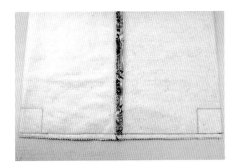

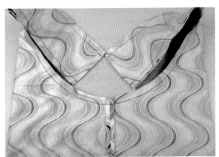

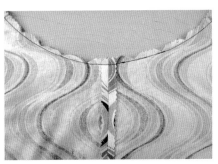

13 **Finish the outer bag.** Repeat Steps 6–9 with the outer bag piece to sew the remaining side and bottom edge and cut and stitch the bottom corners.

14 **Attach the lining.** Nest the outer bag inside the lining with right sides facing. Align the seams, the raw top edges, and the strap edges and pin the pieces in place. Stitch around the top edge and long strap edges using a ½" (1.5cm) seam allowance. Leave the short ends of the straps raw.

15 **Notch the seam allowances.** Notch the seam allowance on the curves of the outer bag. Trim the remaining portions of the seam allowance with pinking shears.

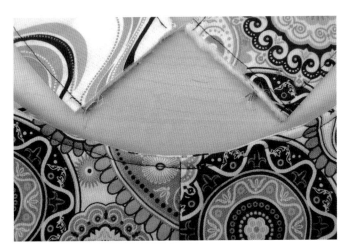

16 **Finish the top edge.** Turn the bag, including the straps, right side out through the opening left in the bottom of the lining for turning. Hand stitch the opening closed using a blind stitch. Nest the lining inside the bag and press the top edge and straps. Using a ¼" (6mm) seam allowance, stitch around the top edge of the bag and side edges of the straps. Leave the ends of the straps raw.

17 **Attach the shoulder pad.** Take one of the bag straps and insert the end into one of the open short ends of the shoulder pad by ½" (1.5cm). Repeat with the remaining strap and other end of the shoulder pad. Pin the straps in place and stitch around all sides of the shoulder pad using a ¼" (6mm) seam allowance.

Peonies & Pearls Messenger Bag

Materials & Tools:

- Fabric A: ⅔ yd. (0.6m) cotton or other (outer bag front/back, outer flap, top strap)
- Fabric B: ⅓ yd. (0.3m) cotton or other (outer bag sides/bottom, bottom strap)
- Fabric C: ⅔ yd. (0.6m) cotton or other (lining front/back, lining sides/bottom, flap lining)
- Medium-weight interfacing: 2 yd. (2m), 17" (43cm) wide
- Medium-weight batting: ⅛ yd. (0.1m)
- Pearl beads or other embellishment of your choice
- Bodkin or safety pin
- Walking foot (optional)

Messenger bags are so versatile, holding everything from school supplies to textbooks to laptops and tablets. They work equally well for both boys and girls. When my son started college, I made this messenger bag for him using black and white houndstooth suiting wool with a black lining. With its floral fabric and pearl bead embellishments, the project shown is a flirty, feminine version.

Cutting Chart

Follow the chart below to cut the pieces for this project from the total fabric yardage indicated in the Materials & Tools list above.

Piece Name	Material to Cut	Size to Cut	Quantity
Outer bag (front/back)	Fabric A	13" x 15" (33 x 38cm)	2
Outer bag (flap)	Fabric A	15" x 16" (38 x 40.5cm)	1
Outer bag (top strap)*	Fabric A	2¾" x 22" (7 x 56cm)	2
Outer bag (sides)	Fabric B	4" x 13" (10 x 33cm)	2
Outer bag (bottom)	Fabric B	4" x 15" (10 x 38cm)	1
Outer bag (bottom strap)*	Fabric B	4½" x 22¾" (11.5 x 57.5cm)	2
Lining (front/back)	Fabric C	13" x 15" (33 x 38cm)	2
Lining (sides)	Fabric C	4" x 13" (10 x 33cm)	2
Lining (bottom)	Fabric C	4" x 15" (10 x 38cm)	1
Lining (flap)	Fabric C	15" x 16" (38 x 40.5cm)	1
Interfacing (front/back)	Medium-weight	12¾" x 14¾" (32.5 x 37.5cm)	2
Interfacing (sides)	Medium-weight	3¾" x 12¾" (9.5 x 32.5cm)	2
Interfacing (bottom)	Medium-weight	3¾" x 14¾" (9.5 x 37.5cm)	1
Interfacing (flap)	Medium-weight	14¾" x 15¾" (37.5 x 40cm)	1
Batting**	Medium-weight	2¾" x 41" (7 x 105cm)	1

*Cut all strap pieces along the grain of the fabric. **Cut the batting in Step 4 after making the top strap.*

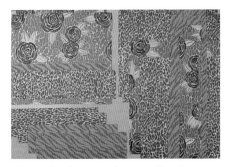

1 **Apply the interfacing.** Cut the fabrics and interfacing to the sizes listed in the cutting chart. Following the manufacturer's instructions, fuse each interfacing piece to the wrong side of its corresponding outer bag piece.

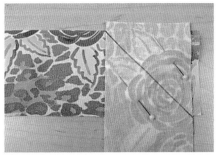

2 **Sew the top strap.** Place the short ends of the two top strap pieces perpendicular to one another with right sides facing. Allow about ¼" (0.5cm) of overlap. Mark a diagonal line that extends roughly from the top corner of the top piece to the bottom corner of the bottom piece. Pin the pieces in place and stitch along this line. Trim the seam allowance with pinking shears and press it to one side.

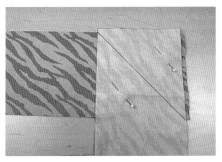

3 **Sew the bottom strap.** Repeat Step 2 to assemble the bottom strap.

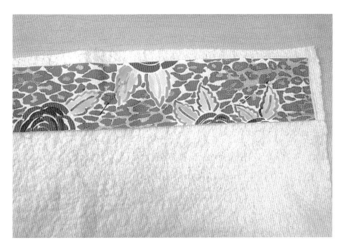

4 **Cut and stitch the batting.** Place the top strap on top of the batting. Pin the strap in place and use it as a pattern to cut out the batting. Repin the batting and strap fabric as necessary. Place a walking foot in your sewing machine and baste the strap fabric to the batting by sewing along both long edges using a ⅛" (3mm) seam allowance.

5 **Sew one side of the straps.** Place the top and bottom strap pieces together with right sides facing. Align the pieces along one long edge. Pin the pieces in place and stitch along the long edge using a ¼" (6mm) seam allowance.

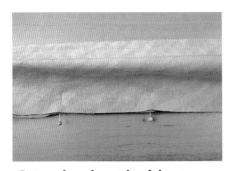

6 **Sew the other side of the straps.** Align and pin the two strap pieces along the open long side. There will be some excess fabric along the center; this is normal. Stitch along this edge using a ¼" (6mm) seam allowance.

7 **Turn and press the strap.** Use a bodkin to turn the strap right side out. If the bodkin is long, stick it into the strap tube and attach it as far from the end as possible. Then thread the bodkin through to the other side of the strap. Position the strap pieces so the top strap is centered along the length of the bottom strap. Press the strap.

8 **Sew the flap.** Place the two flap pieces together with right sides facing and pin them in place. Using a ½" (1.5cm) seam allowance, stitch around the side and bottom edges, leaving the top (15" [38cm] side) open. Trim the seam allowances with pinking shears, clip the corners, and turn the flap right side out. Press the flap.

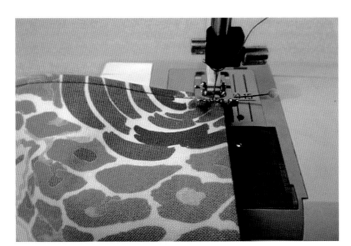

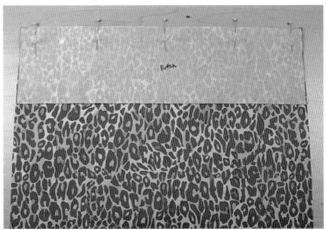

9 **Finish the flap.** Topstitch around the side and bottom edges of the flap using a ⅛" (3mm) seam allowance. Use the pin pull trick (see page 116) on the corners as needed. Embellish the flap as desired. Pearl beads were stitched onto the project shown to accent the flowers in the fabric design.

10 **Begin attaching the lining bottom.** Place the lining bottom piece and the lining front piece together with right sides facing. Align the pieces along one long edge. Pin the pieces in place and stitch along the long edge using a ½" (1.5cm) seam allowance, starting and stopping the stitching ½" (1.5cm) from each end. You can measure and mark the ½" (1.5cm) start and stop points if desired for accuracy.

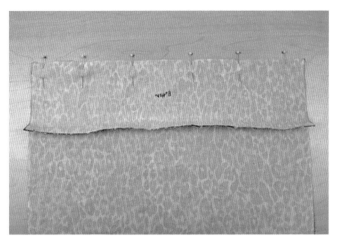

11 Finish attaching the lining bottom. Repeat Step 10 to attach the lining back piece to the remaining long side of the bottom lining piece. When stitching the pieces together, leave a 4" (10cm) opening for turning. Remember to backstitch on each side of the opening for turning.

12 Begin attaching the side pieces. Pin the short end of one lining side piece to one of the short ends of the lining bottom piece with right sides facing. Repeat to pin the remaining side piece to the remaining short end of the bottom piece. Place pins to mark the seams where the front and back pieces are joined to the bottom piece. Sew the side pieces to the bottom piece, stitching from pin to pin.

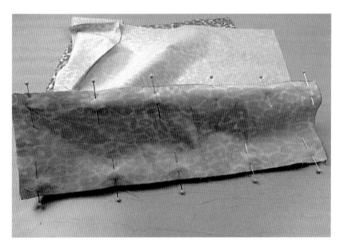

13 Pin and sew the side pieces. Pin the edges of the side pieces to the front and back pieces. Start by aligning and pinning the top corners of each side piece to the corresponding corners of the front and back pieces with right sides facing. Then, pin the edges of the side pieces to the corresponding edges of the front and back pieces working down from the top corners. Using a ½" (1.5cm) seam allowance, stitch along all the pinned edges to attach the side pieces to the front and back pieces. Trim all the seam allowances.

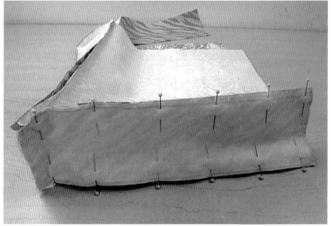

14 Assemble the outer bag. Repeat the same basic procedure used to assemble the bag lining to assemble the outer bag. Stitch the front and back pieces to the long edges of the bottom piece (do not leave an opening for turning). Stitch the side pieces to the short ends of the bottom piece. Stitch the edges of the side pieces to the corresponding edges of the front and back pieces. Trim the seam allowances and turn the outer bag right side out.

15 **Baste the strap.** Pin the strap ends to the outer bag, aligning the short ends of the strap with the top edges of the bag sides. Position the strap so the top strap is facing the right side of the outer bag. Make sure the strap is not twisted. Baste the strap ends in place using a ¼" (6mm) seam allowance.

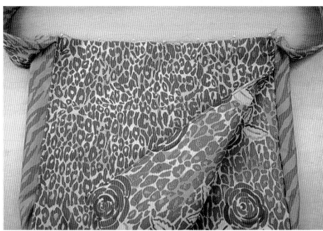

16 **Baste the flap.** Pin the flap to the outer bag, aligning the raw top edge of the flap with the top edge of the bag back. Pin the pieces together with right sides facing. Baste the flap in place using a ¼" (6mm) seam allowance.

17 **Attach the lining.** Nest the outer bag inside the lining with right sides facing. Align the corner seams and the raw top edges and pin the pieces in place. Stitch around the top edge of the bag using a ½" (1.5cm) seam allowance. Trim the seam allowance with pinking shears.

18 **Finish the bag.** Turn the bag right side out through the opening left in the bottom of the lining for turning. Hand stitch the opening closed using a blind stitch. Nest the lining inside the bag and press the top edge. Using a ⅛" (3mm) seam allowance, stitch around the top edge of the bag.

Mod Monogram Backpack

Materials & Tools:

- Fabric A: ½ yd. (0.5m) cotton or other (outer bag front/back, outer bag sides/bottom)
- Fabric B: ⅓ yd. (0.3m) cotton or other (handle, top/bottom straps, utility strap)
- Fabric C: ⅓ yd. (0.3m) or fat eighth cotton or other (flap)
- Fabric D: ½ yd. (0.5m) cotton or other (lining front/back, lining sides/bottom)
- Medium-weight interfacing: 2 yd. (2m), 17" (43cm) wide

- Felt for appliqué: 6" (15cm) square or assorted remnants
- Fusible webbing for appliqué
- Embroidery floss
- Circle template: 4½" (11.5cm) diameter
- 2 plastic strap adjusters: 1½" (38mm) wide
- 2 plastic loops: 1½" (38mm) wide
- 2 sew-in snaps

You will never find an off-the-shelf backpack as cute as this one! It features a felt monogram with embroidery. Refer to the patterns section on page 118 for the full alphabet, or create your own pattern using your favorite font.

Cutting Chart

Follow the chart below to cut the pieces for this project from the total fabric yardage indicated in the Materials & Tools list above.

Piece Name	Material to Cut	Size to Cut	Quantity
Outer bag (front/back)	Fabric A	11" x 14" (28 x 35.5cm)	2
Outer bag (sides)	Fabric A	5" x 14" (12.5 x 35.5cm)	2
Outer bag (bottom)	Fabric A	5" x 11" (12.5 x 28cm)	1
Outer bag (handle)*	Fabric B	4" x 6" (10 x 15cm)	1
Outer bag (top straps)*	Fabric B	3½" x 34" (9 x 86.5cm)	2
Outer bag (bottom straps)*	Fabric B	3½" x 3" (9 x 7.5cm)	2
Outer bag (utility strap)*	Fabric B	1" x 5" (2.5 x 12.5cm)	1
Outer bag (flap)	Fabric C	11" x 13" (28 x 33cm)	2
Lining (front/back)	Fabric D	11" x 14" (28 x 35.5cm)	2
Lining (sides)	Fabric D	5" x 14" (12.5 x 35.5cm)	2
Lining (bottom)	Fabric D	5" x 11" (12.5 x 28cm)	1
Interfacing (front/back)	Medium-weight	10¾" x 13¾" (27.5 x 35cm)	2
Interfacing (sides)	Medium-weight	4¾" x 13¾" (12 x 35cm)	2
Interfacing (bottom)	Medium-weight	4¾" x 10¾" (12 x 27.5cm)	1
Interfacing (top straps)	Medium-weight	3¼" x 33¾" (8.5 x 85.5cm)	2
Interfacing (bottom straps)	Medium-weight	3¼" x 2¾" (8.5 x 7cm)	2
Interfacing (flap)	Medium-weight	10¾" x 12¾" (12 x 32.5cm)	1

Cut all straps along the grain of the fabric.

1 **Apply the interfacing.** Following the manufacturer's instructions, fuse each interfacing strap piece to the wrong side of its corresponding outer bag strap piece.

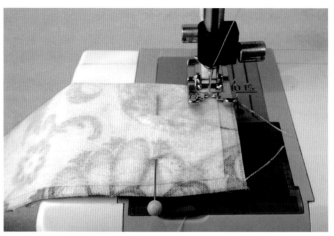

2 **Stitch the top straps.** Take the outer bag top straps and fold each one in half lengthwise with right sides facing. Pin them in place. Using a ¼" (6mm) seam allowance, stitch along one open short end and the long open edge of each strap piece. Leave the remaining short end open. Clip the corners, turn the straps right side out, and press.

3 **Stitch the bottom straps.** Take the outer bag bottom straps and fold each one in half, bringing the 3" (7.5cm) edges together with right sides facing. Pin them in place. Using a ¼" (6mm) seam allowance, stitch along the long open edge of each strap piece, leaving the short ends open. Turn the straps right side out and press them.

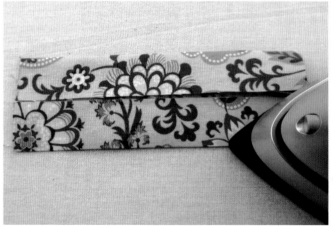

4 **Stitch the handle.** Fold the outer fabric handle in half lengthwise with wrong sides facing and press the fold in place. Open the strap and fold each long edge in until it meets the center crease. Press these folds in place. Fold the strap in half lengthwise along the center crease as before. Stitch along the long open edge using a ⅛" (3mm) seam allowance. Leave the short ends raw.

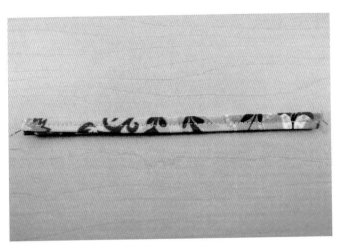

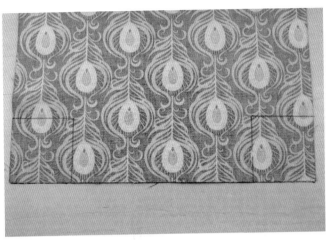

5 **Stitch the utility strap.** Repeat Step 4 with the outer fabric utility strap.

6 **Prepare the flap.** Following the manufacturer's instructions, fuse the interfacing flap piece to the wrong side of one of the flap pieces. Place the flap front and back pieces together with right sides facing. Mark 2¼" (5.5cm) squares in each of the bottom corners (on one 11" [28cm] side).

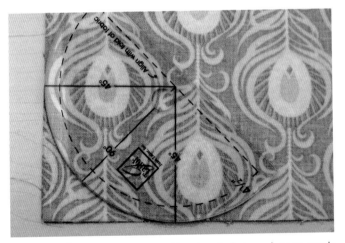

8 **Embellish the flap.** Embellish the front of the flap as desired. This project features a hand-embroidered monogram that was attached to the flap using fusible webbing.

7 **Mark the corner curves.** Use the circle template to mark curves in the bottom corners of the flap. Then cut along the marks to create the curved corners.

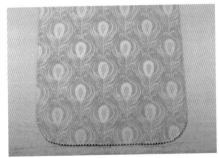

9 **Sew the flap.** Pin the front and back flap pieces together with right sides facing. Using a ½" (1.5cm) seam allowance, sew around the side and bottom edges, leaving the top (11" [28cm] side) open. Trim the selvages with pinking shears, turn the flap right side out, and press it.

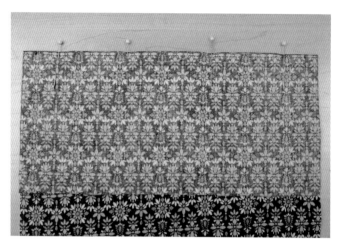

10 **Begin attaching the lining bottom.** Place the lining bottom piece and the lining front piece together with right sides facing. Align the pieces along one 11" (28cm) edge. Pin the pieces in place and stitch along the edge using a ½" (1.5cm) seam allowance, starting and stopping the stitching ½" (1.5cm) from each end. If desired, you can measure and mark the ½" (1.5cm) start and stop points.

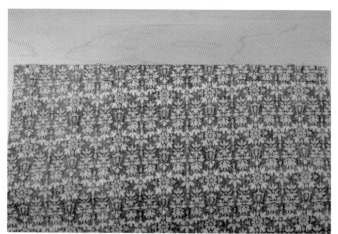

11 **Finish attaching the lining bottom.** Repeat Step 10 to attach the lining back piece to the remaining long side of the bottom lining piece. When stitching the pieces together, leave a 3" (7.5cm) opening for turning. Remember to backstitch on each side of the opening for turning. Press the bottom seams outward.

12 **Begin attaching the side pieces.** Pin the short end of one lining side piece to one of the short ends of the lining bottom piece with right sides facing. Repeat to pin the remaining side piece to the remaining short end of the bottom piece. Place pins to mark the seams where the front and back pieces are joined to the bottom piece. Using a ½" (1.5cm) seam allowance, sew the side pieces to the bottom piece, stitching from pin to pin.

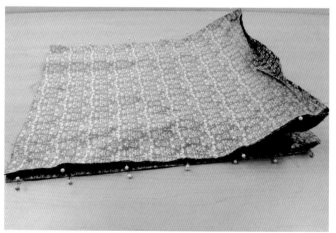

13 **Pin and sew the side pieces.** Pin the edges of the side pieces to the front and back pieces. Start by aligning and pinning the top corners of each side piece to the corresponding corners of the front and back pieces with right sides facing. Then, pin the edges of the side pieces to the corresponding edges of the front and back pieces working down from the top corners. Using a ½" (1.5cm) seam allowance, stitch along all the pinned edges to attach the side pieces to the front and back pieces. Trim all the seam allowances.

14 **Apply the interfacing.** Following the manufacturer's instructions, fuse each interfacing piece to the wrong side of its corresponding outer bag piece.

15 **Baste the bottom straps.** Thread each bottom strap piece through a plastic loop, folding the strap in half around one of the loop's sides. Pin the strap ends to the right side of the outer bag bottom piece. Align the raw ends of the straps with one of the long edges of the bottom piece, positioning each strap 1½" (4cm) in from the side edges. Baste the straps in place using a ¼" (6mm) seam allowance.

16 **Begin attaching the outer bag bottom.** Repeat Step 10 with the outer bag pieces to attach the long edge of the bottom piece with the straps attached to a corresponding edge of the back piece.

17 **Prepare the handle.** Fold each end of the handle down from the center point to create an arrow shape. Press the folds in place to hold the shape.

18 **Baste the handle and top straps.** Pin the ends of the top straps and the handle to the right side of the back piece. Align the short ends of the strap pieces with the top edge of the back piece. Position the top straps 1½" (4cm) in from each side, and center the handle. Baste everything in place using a ¼" (6mm) seam allowance.

19 **Finish attaching the outer bag bottom.** Repeat Step 11 with the outer bag pieces to attach the remaining long edge of the bottom piece to a corresponding edge of the front piece. Do not leave an opening for turning. Press the seams on the bottom piece outward.

20 **Baste the utility strap.** Draw a line across one of the outer bag side pieces, parallel to one short end, 1 ½" (4cm) from the edge. Mark the line on the right side of the fabric. Using this mark, position the utility strap across the side piece, parallel to the short end. Using a ¼" (6mm) seam allowance, baste the short ends of the utility strap in place on the side piece.

21 **Begin attaching the side pieces.** Repeat Step 12 with the outer bag pieces to attach the side pieces to the short ends of the bottom piece.

22 **Pin and sew the side pieces.** Repeat Step 13 with the outer bag pieces to pin and sew the edges of the side pieces to the front and back pieces. Trim all the seam allowances with pinking shears and turn the bag right side out.

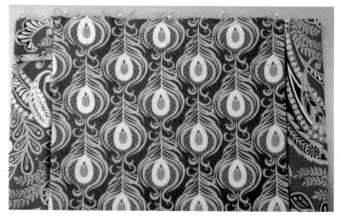

23 **Baste the flap.** Pin the flap to the outer bag, aligning the raw top edge of the flap with the top edge of the bag back. Pin the pieces together with right sides facing, centering the flap. Baste the flap in place using a ¼" (6mm) seam allowance.

24 **Attach the lining.** Nest the outer bag inside the lining with right sides facing. Align the corner seams and the raw top edges and pin the pieces in place. Stitch around the top edge of the bag using a ½" (1.5cm) seam allowance. Trim the seam allowance with pinking shears.

25 **Finish the top edge.** Turn the bag right side out through the opening left in the bottom of the lining for turning. Do not stitch the opening closed yet. Nest the lining inside the bag and press the top edge. Using a ⅛" (3mm) seam allowance, stitch around the top edge of the bag.

26 **Finish the straps.** Thread the finished end of each top strap through a strap adjuster and then through the plastic loop attached to the corresponding bottom strap. Thread the finished end of each strap back through the strap adjuster. Fold over each end by 1½" (4cm) and stitch it in place.

27 **Finish the bag.** Hand sew snaps to the bottom corners on the front of the bag by reaching through the turning hole in the lining. Sew the corresponding snap pieces to the bottom corners of the back of the flap. Fold the flap closed over the front of the bag if necessary to help with the snap placement. Hand stitch the opening in the lining closed using a blind stitch.

Zen Yoga Bag

Materials & Tools:

- Fabric A: 1 yd. (1m) cotton or other (outer bag, flower pin layer 3)
- Fabric B: 1 yd. (1m) cotton or other (lining, flower pin layer 1)
- Fabric C: ½ yd. (0.5m) cotton or other (pocket, handles, button loop, flower pin layer 2)
- Craft weight, fusible interfacing: 1 yd. (1m), 17" (43cm) wide
- Elastic: 6" (15cm), ¾" (19mm) wide
- Bodkin or safety pin
- Walking foot (optional)
- Button: 2" (50mm) diameter
- Circle templates: 7½" (19cm) and 4½" (11.5cm) diameter
- Point turner tool
- Fabric glue
- Jewelry pin back
- Button or decorative centerpiece (for flower pin)
- Felt: 3" (7.5cm) square

Stand out in a crowd with this elegant and serene yoga bag, perfect for carrying your mat, towel, and a change of clothes to your favorite workout. It also features an exterior water bottle pocket with an elastic top to hold your drink of choice. Make the accompanying flower pin to add an extra-special embellishment.

Cutting Chart

Follow the chart below to cut the pieces for this project from the total fabric yardage indicated in the Materials & Tools list above.

Piece Name	Material to Cut	Size to Cut	Quantity
Outer Bag	Fabric A	31" x 14" (78.5 x 35.5cm)	2
Flower pin (layer 3)	Fabric A	4½" x 4½" (11.5 x 11.5cm)	2
Lining	Fabric B	31" x 14" (78.5 x 35.5cm)	2
Flower pin (layer 1)	Fabric B	7½" x 7½" (19 x 19cm)	1
Pocket	Fabric C	18" x 9½" (45.5 x 24cm)	1
Handles	Fabric C	5" x 26" (12.5 x 66cm)	2
Button loop (cut along the grain)	Fabric C	2½" x 7" (6.5 x 18cm)	1
Flower pin (layer 2)	Fabric C	7½" x 7½" (19 x 19cm)	2
Interfacing	Craft weight, fusible	30¾" x 13¾" (78 x 35cm)	2
Elastic		¾" x 5½" (19mm x 14cm)	1
Flower pin felt		2½" x 2½" (6.5 x 6.5cm)	1

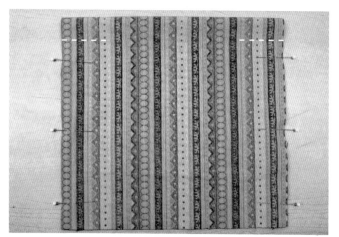

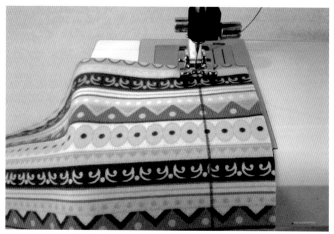

1 **Prepare the pocket.** Fold the pocket in half widthwise with right sides facing so it is 9" x 9½" (23 x 24cm). Pin the fabric in place. Starting 1" (2.5cm) from the fold, stitch along one of the open 9" (23cm) sides using a ¼" (6mm) seam allowance. Repeat on the other 9" (23cm) side, leaving the bottom edge (opposite the fold) open.

2 **Stitch the elastic casing.** Turn the pocket right side out, and press it. Form the elastic casing by stitching along the folded edge of the pocket, ⅞" (2cm) from the fold.

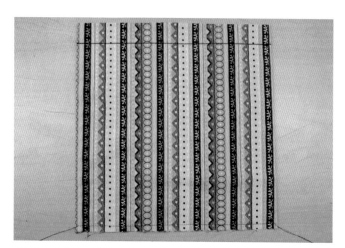

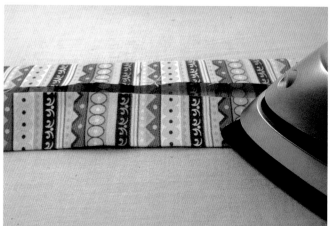

3 **Sew the gathering stitches.** Set the stitch length on your machine to 5. Leaving long starting tails with both your machine and bobbin threads, stitch across the bottom of the pocket, ⅜" (1cm) from the edge. Leave long ending tails with both your machine and bobbin threads.

4 **Prepare the handles.** Fold each handle piece in half lengthwise with wrong sides facing and press the fold in place. Open each handle piece and fold each long edge in until it meets the center crease. Press these folds in place. Fold each handle in half lengthwise along the center crease as before. Stitch along the long open edge using a ⅛" (3mm) seam allowance. Leave the short ends raw.

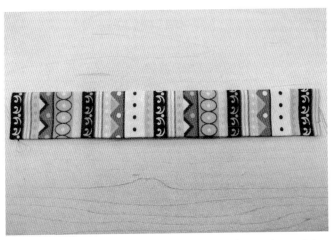

5 **Prepare the button loop.** Fold over the long edges of the button loop piece by ¼" (6mm). Press the folds in place. Fold the button loop piece in half, bringing the pressed edges together with wrong sides facing. Press the fold in place, and then stitch along the long open edge using a ⅛" (3mm) seam allowance. Leave the short ends raw.

6 **Stitch the button loop.** Fold each end of the button loop strip down from the center point to create an arrow shape. Press the folds in place to hold the shape. Stitch along the edges of the triangle shape using a ⅛" (3mm) seam allowance. Use the pin pull trick (page 116) if necessary.

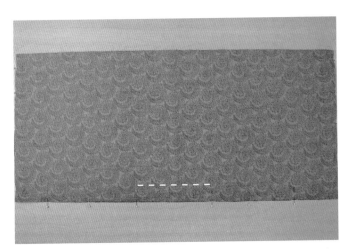

7 **Stitch the lining.** Pin the two lining pieces together with right sides facing. Using a ½" (1.5cm) seam allowance, sew along the side and bottom edges, leaving the top (long side) open. Leave a 6" (15cm) opening for turning along the center of the bottom edge. Remember to backstitch on both sides of the opening for turning.

8 **Cut the corners.** Draw 2½" (6.5cm) squares in the bottom corners of the lining. Then cut out the squares.

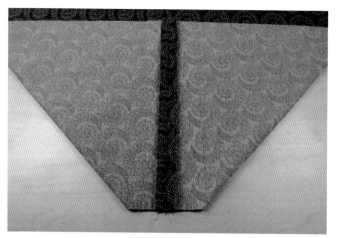

9 **Fold and stitch the corners.** Press the lining seams open. Fold the lining fabric so the side seams align with the bottom seam and the bottom corners form straight raw edges as shown. Pin the corners in place, and then stitch straight along the raw edges using a ½" (1.5cm) seam allowance.

10 **Apply the interfacing.** Following the manufacturer's instructions, fuse an interfacing piece to the wrong side of each outer bag piece.

11 **Stitch the outer bag.** Place the outer bag pieces together with right sides facing and pin them in place. Place a walking foot in your sewing machine and sew around the side and bottom edges using a ½" (1.5cm) seam allowance. Leave the top (long side) open.

12 **Cut the corners.** Draw 2½" (6.5cm) squares in the bottom corners of the outer bag. Then cut out the squares.

Tip

Use a walking foot for Step 11 if you have one available. This foot can better grip and move the heavy interfacing applied to the outer bag pieces than a standard sewing machine foot.

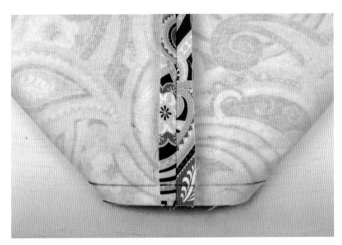

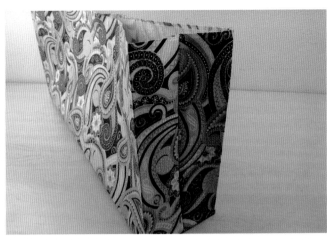

13 **Fold and stitch one corner.** Press the outer bag seams open. Fold the fabric so the side seams align with the bottom seam and the bottom corners form straight raw edges as shown. Pin the corners in place, and then stitch straight along only one of the corners using a ½" (1.5cm) seam allowance. Mark the ½" (1.5cm) seam allowance on the other corner, but leave it unsewn. Pin it closed instead and turn the bag right side out.

14 **Mark and press the corner creases.** Measure and draw marks 2½" (6.5cm) to each side of both side seams on the outer bag. This marks the corner creases of the bag. Fold the bag along the marks you made and press the folds in place.

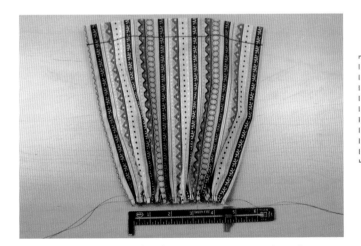

Tip

When gathering fabric, always pull on the bobbin thread instead of the machine thread. The bobbin thread is easier to pull and less likely to break than the machine thread.

15 **Gather the pocket bottom.** Secure the threads on the left side of the pocket bottom. Pull on the bobbin thread on the right side of the pocket. This will begin to gather the fabric. Continue pulling and gathering the pocket bottom until it is about 4½" (11.5cm) wide.

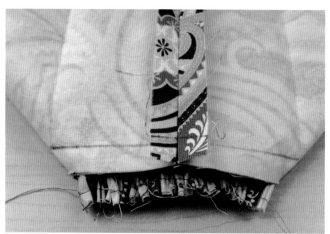

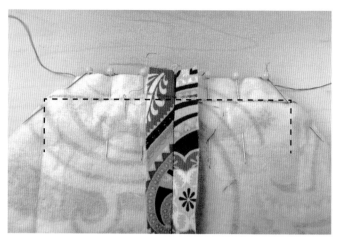

16 **Position the pocket.** Turn the outer bag inside out. Remove the pins from the open corner. Fold the fabric so the side seam and bottom seam align and the open corner forms a straight raw edge as shown. Place the pocket inside the bag, inserting the bottom gathered edge into the open corner. Align the raw edge of the pocket bottom with the raw straight edge of the bag corner.

17 **Stitch the pocket.** Pin the pocket in place on the bag's corner. Adjust the gathering at the pocket bottom to make sure the pocket reaches to both sides of the bag corner at the ½" (1.5cm) seam allowance mark. Stitch straight across the corner at the ½" (1.5cm) mark.

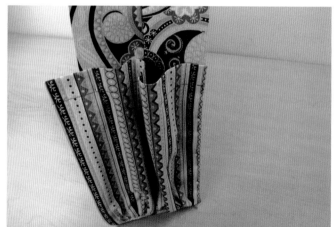

18 **Check the pocket placement.** Remove the pins and turn the bag right side out to check the position of the pocket. Make sure the pocket fabric reaches to both sides of the bag corner. Once you're satisfied, trim away the gathering threads and trim the seam allowance with pinking shears.

19 **Pin the pocket.** Turn the outer bag right side out. Starting from the bottom right side of the pocket and working upward, pin the right side of the pocket to the right side of the bag, matching up the edge of the pocket with the bag's corner crease.

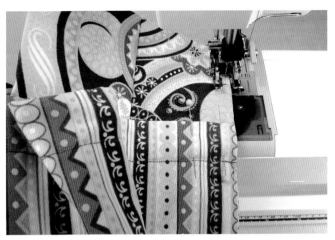

20 **Add and cover the elastic.** Use a safety pin or bodkin to thread the elastic into the casing at the top of the pocket from the right side. Align the right end of the elastic with the right edge of the pocket, just inside the casing, and pin it in place. Using the tip of a straight pin, pull the loose inseam fabric out of the right end of the casing and then tuck it back in again to cover the end of the elastic.

21 **Stitch the pocket.** Using a ⅛" (3mm) seam allowance, topstitch along the corner crease of the bag with the right side of the pocket pinned to it, stitching from top to bottom. This will attach the pocket and elastic in the process.

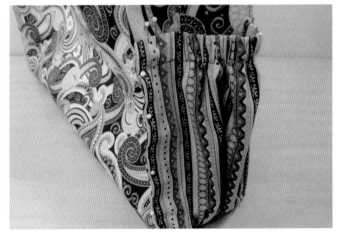

22 **Finish the pocket.** Repeat Steps 19–20 to pin the left side of the pocket and elastic in place and cover the left side of the elastic. Before stitching, make sure the top left corner of the pocket is at the same height as the top right corner. Using a ⅛" (3mm) seam allowance, topstitch along the corner crease of the bag with the left side of the pocket pinned to it, stitching from bottom to top.

23 **Stitch the remaining corner creases.** Using a ⅛" (3mm) seam allowance, topstitch along the remaining two corner creases on the side of the bag without the pocket.

Tip

Decide how you plan to carry your yoga bag before placing the button loop. For example, if you want to carry the bag on your left shoulder with the bottle pocket at the front, you'll want to attach the button loop to the side of the bag that will be closest to your body and the button to the side that will be furthest from your body.

24 **Baste the handles and button loop.** Pin the handle ends to the outer bag, aligning the short ends of the handles with the top edge of the bag, 7¾" (19.5cm) in from each corner of the bag. Pin the button loop onto the back side of the bag, centered along the top edge with the triangle shape face down. Align the short raw end with the top edge of the bag. Baste the handle and button loop ends in place using a ¼" (6mm) seam allowance.

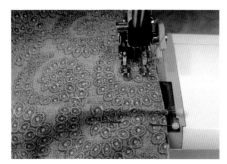

25 **Attach the lining.** Nest the outer bag inside the lining with right sides facing. Align the side seams and the raw top edges and pin the pieces in place. Stitch around the top edge of the bag using a ½" (1.5cm) seam allowance. Pinch the lining fabric over the corner creases to make sewing around the corners easier. Trim the seam allowance with pinking shears.

26 **Finish the top edge.** Turn the bag right side out through the opening left in the bottom of the lining for turning. Do not stitch the opening closed yet. Nest the lining inside the bag and press the top edge. Using a ⅛" (3mm) seam allowance, stitch around the top edge of the bag.

27 **Finish the bag.** Hand sew the button centered on the front of the bag by reaching through the turning hole in the lining. The center of the button should be about 2" (5cm) from the top edge of the bag. Fold the button loop over onto the front of the bag if necessary to help with the button placement. Hand stitch the opening in the lining closed using a blind stitch.

Flower Pin

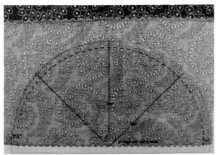

1 **Cut out the circle.** Fold the fabric for layer 1 in half with right sides facing. Fold your circle template in half if necessary and align the folded edge with the folded edge of the fabric. Trace the half circle onto the fabric, and then cut it out.

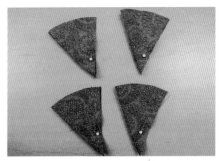

2 **Cut and fold the quarters.** Cut the circle into four equal quarters. Fold each quarter in half, bringing the straight edges together, with right sides facing. Pin the quarters in place and stitch along the straight open edge using a ⅛" (3mm) seam allowance to create four cone shapes.

3 **Prepare the cones.** Trim the seam allowance at the tip of each cone and turn them right side out using a point turner tool. Press the cones flat with the seam centered on the back side.

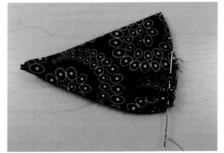

4 **Gather the first petal.** Using a sewing needle and doubled thread, sew a gathering stitch along the raw curved edge of one of the cones to close it. Gather the fabric at the curved edge as tightly as possible to form the cone into a petal shape. Make a knot to hold the gathers in place.

5 **Gather the second petal.** Using the thread still attached to the first petal, repeat Step 4 with another cone to form the second petal. Position the second petal right next to the first petal, gather the fabric as tightly as possible, and make a knot to hold everything in place.

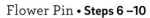

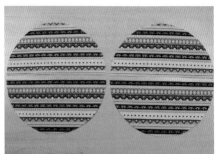

6 Finish the petals. Repeat to gather the remaining two petals. Place the first and last petals next to one another and stitch the gathered ends together so all four petals form a circle.

7 Cut out the circles. Repeat Step 1 with the layer 2 fabric pieces to cut out two 7½" (19cm)-diameter circles. Cut each circle in half so you have four equal pieces.

8 Prepare the cones. Repeat Steps 2 and 3 to fold and stitch the circle halves into cones, turn them right side out, and press them. Use a ¼" (6mm) seam allowance when stitching the layer 2 cones. When you press the cones, the back sides should be a little longer than the front sides as shown.

9 Stitch the center. Take each cone and align the raw edges. Sew a 1½"–2" (4–5cm) line down the center of each cone, starting at the raw edge and moving toward the point. This will cause the cone to pucker on the back side (shown) and curl on the front side.

10 Create the second layer. Repeat Steps 4–6 to gather and stitch the layer 2 petals together in a circle with the curled front sides facing up.

11 **Create the third layer.** Repeat Steps 7–10 with two 4½" (11.5cm) circles cut from the layer 3 fabric pieces to form the third layer of petals.

12 **Attach the pin back.** Cut a 2½" (6.5cm)-diameter circle of felt. Hand stitch the jewelry pin onto the back of the circle. Using fabric glue, glue the felt piece to the back of the first layer of petals with the pin facing out.

13 **Attach the second and third layers.** Using a generous amount of fabric glue, attach the second layer of petals to the front of the first layer. Then attach the third layer of petals on top of the second.

14 **Attach the embellishment.** Glue the center embellishment in place in the center of the flower. Use a vintage button or an earring that has lost its mate for a completely unique piece!

Travel Drawstring Bag Set

Bag 1: 13½" x 20" (34 x 51cm)	Bag 2: 12" x 18" (30.5 x 45.5cm)	Bag 3: 10 ½" x 15" (26.5 x 38cm)			
13½" x 4½" (34 x 29cm)	12" x 4" (30.5 x 10cm)	10½" x 3½" (26.5 x 9cm)			

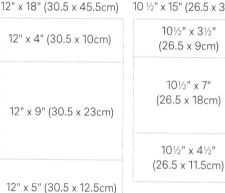

Bag 4: 9" x 13" (23 x 33cm)

Bag 5: 7½" x 10½" (19 x 26.5cm)

Bag 6: 6" x 8½" (15 x 21.5cm)

13½" x 10" (34 x 25.5cm)

12" x 9" (30.5 x 23cm)

10½" x 7" (26.5 x 18cm)

9" x 3" (23 x 7.5cm)

7½" x 2½" (19 x 6.5cm)

6" x 2" (15 x 5cm)

7½" x 5" (19 x 12.5cm)

6" x 4" (15 x 10cm)

9" x 6" (23 x 15cm)

10½" x 4½" (26.5 x 11.5cm)

6" x 2½" (15 x 6.5cm)

13½" x 5½" (34 x 14cm)

12" x 5" (30.5 x 12.5cm)

7½" x 3" (19 x 7.5cm)

9" x 4" (23 x 10cm)

Materials & Tools:

- Fabric A: ½ yd. (0.5m) cotton (Bag #1 top/bottom accent)
- Fabric B: ⅓ yd. (0.3m) cotton (Bag #1 main bag)
- Fabric C: ⅔ yd. (0.6m) cotton (Bag #1 lining)
- Fabric D: ½ yd. (0.5m) cotton (Bag #2 top/bottom accent)
- Fabric E: ⅓ yd. (0.3m) cotton (Bag #2 main bag)
- Fabric F: ⅔ yd. (0.6m) cotton (Bag #2 lining)
- Fabric G: ½ yd. (0.5m) cotton (Bag #3 top/bottom accent)
- Fabric H: ¼ yd. (0.25m) cotton (Bag #3 main bag)
- Fabric I: ½ yd. (0.5m) cotton (Bag #3 lining)
- Fabric J: ½ yd. (0.5m) cotton (Bag #4 top/bottom accent)
- Fabric K: ¼ yd. (0.25m) cotton (Bag #4 main bag)
- Fabric L: ½ yd. (0.5m) cotton (Bag #4 lining)

- Fabric M: ⅓ yd. (0.3m) cotton (Bag #5 top/bottom accent)
- Fabric N: ¼ yd. (0.25m) cotton (Bag #5 main bag)
- Fabric O: ⅓ yd. (0.3m) cotton (Bag #5 lining)
- Fabric P: ⅛ yd. (0.1m) cotton (Bag #6 top/bottom accent)
- Fabric Q: ¼ yd. (0.25m) cotton (Bag #6 main bag)
- Fabric R: ⅓ yd. (0.3m) cotton (Bag #6 lining)
- Velvet or grosgrain ribbon: 6 yd. (5.5m), ⅝" (1.5cm) wide
- Bodkin or safety pin
- Beads of your choice: 2 per bag
- Turning stick

An organized traveler is a happy traveler! I'd taken dozens of trips around the world before I discovered the secret to keeping my suitcase organized. I received a set of three zippered pouches as a gift. They are specially designed for organizing items inside your suitcase, and now I never travel without them. This set of bags uses the same concept. The various sizes are perfect for organizing jewelry, socks, underwear, accessories, and shoes. When you're not traveling, use the bags to keep dresser drawers, cars, and kids' bedrooms organized. Choose two coordinating fabrics for the outside of each bag, and a third fabric for the lining. This set uses different fabrics from the same collection for a colorful array.

Follow the chart below to cut the pieces for this project from the total fabric yardage indicated in the Materials & Tools list on page 66.

Piece Name	Material to Cut	Size to Cut	Quantity
Bag #1: 13½" x 20" (34 x 51cm)			
Top accent	Fabric A	14½" x 5½" (37 x 14cm)	2
Bottom accent	Fabric A	14½" x 12" (37 x 30.5cm)	1
Main bag	Fabric B	14½" x 11" (37 x 28cm)	2
Lining	Fabric C	14½" x 21" (37 x 53.5cm)	2
Ribbon	Velvet or grosgrain	⅝" x 43" (1.5mm x 110cm)	2
Bag #2: 12" x 18" (30.5 x 45.5cm)			
Top accent	Fabric D	13" x 5" (33 x 12.5cm)	2
Bottom accent	Fabric D	13" x 11" (33 x 28cm)	1
Main bag	Fabric E	13" x 10" (33 x 25.5cm)	2
Lining	Fabric F	13" x 19" (33 x 48.5cm)	2
Ribbon	Velvet or grosgrain	⅝" x 40" (1.5mm x 100cm)	2
Bag #3: 10½" x 15" (26.5 x 38cm)			
Top accent	Fabric G	11½" x 4½" (29 x 11.5cm)	2
Bottom accent	Fabric G	11½" x 10" (29 x 25.5cm)	1
Main bag	Fabric H	11½" x 8" (29 x 20.5cm)	2
Lining	Fabric I	11½" x 16" (29 x 40.5cm)	2
Ribbon	Velvet or grosgrain	⅝" x 37" (1.5mm x 95cm)	2
Bag #4: 9" x 13" (23 x 33cm)			
Top accent	Fabric J	10" x 4" (25.5 x 10cm)	2
Bottom accent	Fabric J	10" x 9" (25.5 x 23cm)	1
Main bag	Fabric K	10" x 7" (25.5 x 18cm)	2
Lining	Fabric L	10" x 14" (25.5 x 35.5cm)	2
Ribbon	Velvet or grosgrain	⅝" x 37" (1.5mm x 95cm)	2
Bag #5: 7½" x 10½" (19 x 26.5cm)			
Top accent	Fabric M	8½" x 3½" (21.5 x 9cm)	2
Bottom accent	Fabric M	8½" x 7" (21.5 x 18cm)	1
Main bag	Fabric N	8½" x 6" (21.5 x 15cm)	2
Lining	Fabric O	8½" x 11½" (21.5 x 29cm)	2
Ribbon	Velvet or grosgrain	⅝" x 31" (1.5mm x 80cm)	2
Bag #6: 6" x 8½" (15 x 21.5cm)			
Top accent	Fabric P	7" x 3" (18 x 7.5cm)	2
Bottom accent	Fabric P	7" x 6" (18 x 15cm)	1
Main bag	Fabric Q	7" x 5" (18 x 12.5cm)	2
Lining	Fabric R	7" x 9½" (18 x 24cm)	2
Ribbon	Velvet or grosgrain	⅝" x 28" (1.5mm x 70cm)	2

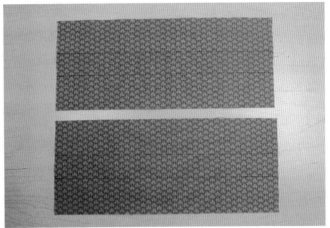

1 **Prepare the pieces.** Cut the pieces for each bag following the cutting chart. Keep all the pieces for each bag grouped together so it's easy to tell each bag apart.

2 **Mark the casing.** Take the two top accent pieces for Bag #1, and mark two parallel lines down the center of each piece. The lines should be 2¼" (5.5cm) in from each long edge and run the length of the fabric as shown. Mark both the front and back sides of the fabric.

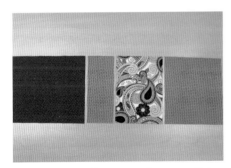

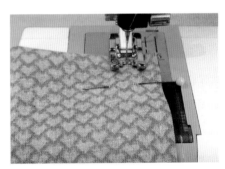

3 **Stitch the first set of pieces.** Take the pieces for Bag #1 and lay them out in the following order, aligning the edges as shown: lining, top accent, main fabric, bottom accent, main fabric, top accent, lining. Using a ½" (1.5cm) seam allowance, stitch the adjoining edges together to form one long strip.

4 **Pin the bag.** Press all the seams open. On the smaller bags, you can press the seams away from the marks for the drawstring casing. Fold the long strip in half widthwise with right sides together, aligning all the seams. Pin the strip in place.

5 **Stitch the bag.** Using a ½" (1.5cm) seam allowance, stitch around all the edges of the bag, leaving a 3" (7.5cm) opening at the short end of the lining for turning. Also skip over the space between the parallel lines marked on the top accent pieces. Backstitch at each line.

6 **Press the bag.** Clip all the corners and press the side seams open. Turn the bag right side out, poking out the corners with your finger or a turning stick, and press it. Hand stitch the opening in the lining closed with a blind stitch.

7 **Check the drawstring casing.** Nest the lining inside the bag and press the top edge. Look into the holes for the drawstring casing and make sure the side seams are pressed back to each side. You should be able to see the lining fabric through the holes.

8 **Sew the drawstring casing.** Sew along the parallel lines you marked on the top accent pieces for the drawstring casing. Start at one drawstring hole and sew all the way around the bag until you reach your starting point. Do this on both lines.

9 **Add the ribbon.** Using a bodkin or safety pin, thread one ribbon through the casing at the top of the bag. Start on the left side, thread the ribbon all the way around the bag, and bring it out on the left side again. Repeat with the second ribbon on the right side of the bag.

10 **Finish the ends.** Finish the ends of each pair of ribbons by adding beads to them, or simply tie each pair together in a knot.

11 **Create the remaining bags.** Repeat these steps to create the remaining five bags. Use the following measurements to mark the drawstring casing on each bag: Bag #2, 2" (5cm); Bag #3, 1¾" (4.5cm); Bag #4, 1½" (4cm); Bag #5, 1¼" (3.5cm); Bag #6, 1" (3cm).

Going Green Reusable Lunch Bag Set

Materials & Tools:
- Fabric A: ½ yd. (0.5m) cotton or other (lunch bag front/back, lunch bag lining)
- Fabric B: ½ yd. (0.5m) cotton or other (sandwich bag lining, snack bag lining)
- Fabric C: ¼ yd. (0.25m) cotton or other (lunch bag flap, sandwich bag flap, snack bag flap)
- Fabric D: ¼ yd. (0.25m) cotton or other (sandwich bag front/back); will yield 2 sandwich bags
- Fabric E: ¼ yd. (0.25m) cotton or other (snack bag front/back); will yield 3+ snack bags
- Heavyweight or craft weight interfacing: 1¼ yd. (1.1m), 17" (43cm) wide
- Hook-and-loop tape: 1" (25mm) wide
- Felt for appliqué
- Embroidery floss

Disposable is out and reusable is in! Send your kids to school or go to work in style with this washable lunch bag set, complete with a sandwich and snack bag. Purchase some extra fabric, and you can make as many snack bags as you want! The set shown was made using 100% quilting cotton, but you can easily substitute this for other fabrics, such as organic canvas, laminated fabric, vinyl, or pastry cloth.

Cutting Chart

Follow the chart below to cut the pieces for this project from the total fabric yardage indicated in the Materials & Tools list above.

Piece Name	Material to Cut	Size to Cut	Quantity
Lunch bag (front/back)	Fabric A	13½" x 13½" (34 x 34cm)	2
Lunch bag lining	Fabric B	13½" x 13½" (34 x 34cm)	2
Sandwich bag lining	Fabric B	8½" x 7½" (21.5 x 19cm)	2
Snack bag lining	Fabric B	7½" x 5" (19 x 12.5cm)	2
Lunch bag (flap)	Fabric C	5½" x 8½" (14 x 21.5cm)	2
Sandwich bag (flap)	Fabric C	6¾" x 4½" (17 x 11.5cm)	2
Snack bag (flap)	Fabric C	7½" x 3" (19 x 7.5cm)	2
Sandwich bag (front/back)	Fabric D	8½" x 7½" (21.5 x 19cm)	2
Snack bag (front/back)	Fabric E	7½" x 5" (19 x 12.5cm)	2
Lunch bag interfacing	Craft/heavyweight	13¼" x 13¼" (33.5 x 33.5cm)	2
Lunch bag hook-and-loop tape		1" x 5" (2.5 x 12.5cm)	1
Sandwich bag hook-and-loop tape		1" x 4" (2.5 x 10cm)	1
Snack bag hook-and-loop tape		1" x 5" (2.5 x 12.5cm)	1

Lunch Bag

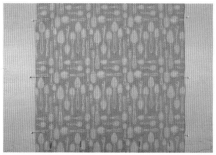

1 **Stitch the lining.** Pin the two lunch bag lining pieces together with right sides facing. Using a ½" (1.5cm) seam allowance, sew along the side and bottom edges, leaving the top open. Leave a 4" (10cm) opening for turning along the center of the bottom edge. Remember to backstitch on both sides of the opening for turning.

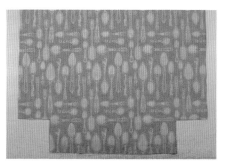

2 **Cut the corners.** Draw 2¼" (5.5cm) squares in the bottom corners of the lining. Then cut out the squares.

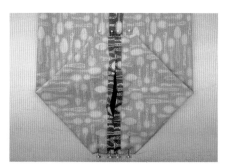

3 **Fold and stitch the corners.** Press the lining seams open. Fold the lining fabric so the side seams align with the bottom seam and the bottom corners form straight raw edges as shown. Pin the corners in place, and then stitch straight along the raw edges using a ½" (1.5cm) seam allowance.

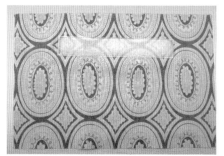

4 **Attach the hook-and-loop tape.** Take the hook side of the hook-and-loop tape and sew it to the right side of one of the lunch bag flap pieces. Position the tape parallel to one of the long sides, about 1" (2.5cm) from the edge, centered from side to side.

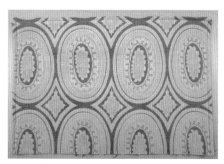

5 **Sew the flap.** Pin the two lunch bag flap pieces together with right sides facing. Using a ½" (1.5cm) seam allowance, sew along the side and top edges, leaving the bottom (without hook-and-loop tape) open. Trim the seam allowances with pinking shears and clip the corners. Turn the flap right side out and press it, being careful not to touch the hook-and-loop tape with the iron. Topstitch around the side and top edges using a ⅛" (3mm) seam allowance. The pin pull trick (page 116) is handy on these corners.

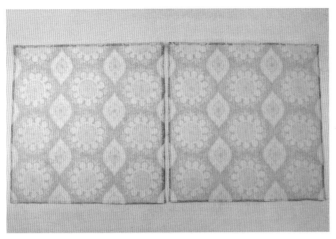

6 Apply the interfacing. Following the manufacturer's instructions, fuse a lunch bag interfacing piece to the wrong side of each lunch bag outer bag piece.

7 Attach the hook-and-loop tape. Sew the loop side of the hook-and-loop tape to the right side of one of the lunch bag outer bag pieces. Position the tape parallel to one of the sides, about 2¾" (7cm) from the edge, centered from side to side.

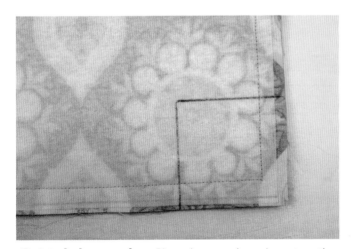

8 Stitch the outer bag. Place the outer bag pieces together with right sides facing and pin them in place. Using a ½" (1.5cm) seam allowance, sew around the side and bottom edges, leaving the top (with hook-and-loop tape) open. Draw 2¼" (7cm) squares in the bottom corners of the outer bag. Then cut out the squares.

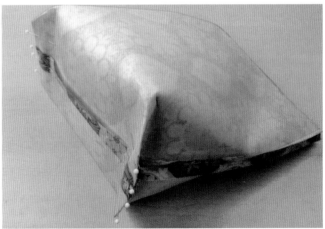

9 Stitch the corners. Press the outer bag seams open. Fold the outer bag pieces so the side seams align with the bottom seam and the bottom corners form straight raw edges. Pin the corners in place, and then stitch straight along the raw edges using a ½" (1.5cm) seam allowance.

10 **Mark the corner creases.** Turn the bag right side out. Measure and draw marks 2¼" (6mm) to each side of both side seams. This marks the corner creases of the bag.

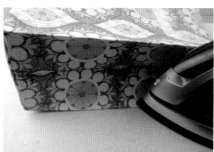

11 **Stitch the corner creases.** Fold the bag along the corner crease marks you made in Step 10. Press the folds in place, and then topstitch along each one using a ¹⁄₁₆" (2mm) seam allowance to hold them in place. You can also topstitch along the bottom edges of the bag if you would like.

12 **Baste the flap.** Pin the flap to the back of the outer bag with the hook-and-loop strip facing up. Align the raw bottom edge of the flap with the top edge of the bag. Baste the flap in place using a ¼" (6mm) seam allowance. If you wish to embellish the outer lunch bag, do it now before you attach the lining in the next step.

13 **Attach the lining.** Nest the outer bag inside the lining with right sides facing. Align the side seams and the raw top edges and pin the pieces in place. Stitch around the top edge of the bag using a ½" (1.5cm) seam allowance. Trim the seam allowance with pinking shears.

14 **Finish the bag.** Turn the bag right side out through the opening left in the bottom of the lining for turning. Hand stitch the opening closed using a blind stitch. Nest the lining inside the bag and press the top edge. Using a ⅛" (3mm) seam allowance, stitch around the top edge of the bag.

Sandwich Bag

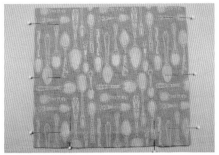

1 Stitch the lining. Pin the two sandwich bag lining pieces together with right sides facing. Using a ½" (1.5cm) seam allowance, sew along the side and bottom edges, leaving the top (7½" [19cm] side) open. Leave a 3" (7.5cm) opening for turning along the center of the bottom edge. Remember to backstitch on both sides of the opening for turning.

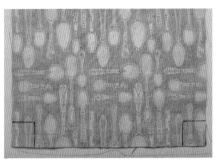

2 Cut the corners. Draw 1" (2.5cm) squares in the bottom corners of the lining. Then cut out the squares.

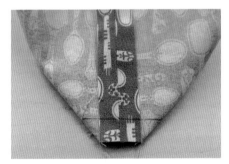

3 Fold and stitch the corners. Press the lining seams open. Fold the lining fabric so the side seams align with the bottom seam and the bottom corners form straight raw edges as shown. Pin the corners in place, and then stitch straight along the raw edges using a ½" (1.5cm) seam allowance.

4 Attach the hook-and-loop tape. Take the hook side of the hook-and-loop tape and sew it to the right side of one of the sandwich bag flap pieces. Position the tape parallel to one of the 6¾" (17cm) sides, about 1" (2.5cm) from the edge, centered from side to side.

5 Sew the flap. Pin the two sandwich bag flap pieces together with right sides facing. Using a ½" (1.5cm) seam allowance, sew along the side and top edges, leaving the bottom (without hook-and-loop tape) open. Trim the seam allowances with pinking shears and clip the corners. Turn the flap right side out and press it, being careful not to touch the hook-and-loop tape with the iron. Topstitch around the side and top edges using a ⅛" (3mm) seam allowance.

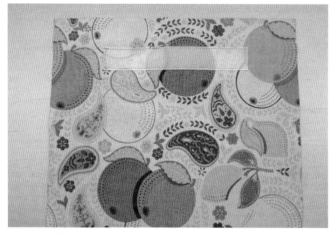

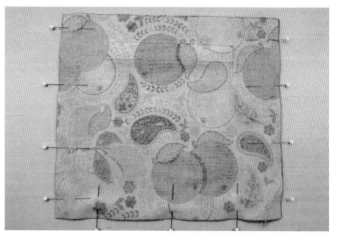

6 **Attach the hook-and-loop tape.** Sew the loop side of the hook-and-loop tape to the right side of one of the sandwich bag outer bag pieces. Position the tape parallel to one of the 7½" (19cm) sides, about 1" (2.5cm) from the edge, centered from side to side.

7 **Stitch the outer bag and corners.** Place the outer bag pieces together with right sides facing and pin them in place. Using a ½" (1.5cm) seam allowance, sew around the side and bottom edges, leaving the top (with hook-and-loop tape) open. Repeat Steps 2–3 to fold and stitch the corners as you did for the lining.

8 **Baste the flap.** Pin the flap to the back of the outer bag with the hook-and-loop strip facing up. Align the raw bottom edge of the flap with the top edge of the bag. Baste the flap in place using a ¼" (6mm) seam allowance.

9 **Attach the lining.** Nest the outer bag inside the lining with right sides facing. Align the side seams and the raw top edges and pin the pieces in place. Stitch around the top edge of the bag using a ½" (1.5cm) seam allowance. Trim the seam allowance with pinking shears.

10 **Finish the bag.** Turn the bag right side out through the opening left in the bottom of the lining for turning. Hand stitch the opening closed using a blind stitch. Nest the lining inside the bag and press the top edge. Using a ⅛" (3mm) seam allowance, stitch around the top edge of the bag.

Snack Bag

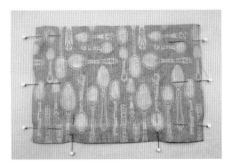

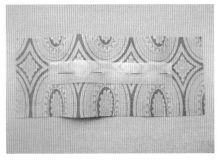

1 **Stitch the lining.** Pin the two snack bag lining pieces together with right sides facing. Using a ½" (1.5cm) seam allowance, sew along the side and bottom edges, leaving the top (long side) open. Leave a 3" (7.5cm) opening for turning along the center of the bottom edge. Remember to backstitch on both sides of the opening for turning.

2 **Attach the hook-and-loop tape.** Take the hook side of the hook-and-loop tape and sew it to the right side of one of the snack bag flap pieces. Position the tape parallel to one of the long sides, about 1" (2.5cm) from the edge, centered from side to side.

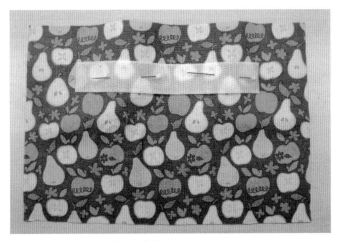

3 **Sew the flap.** Pin the two snack bag flap pieces together with right sides facing. Using a ½" (1.5cm) seam allowance, sew along the side and top edges, leaving the bottom (without hook-and-loop tape) open. Trim the seam allowances with pinking shears and clip the corners. Turn the flap right side out and press it, being careful not to touch the hook-and-loop tape with the iron. Topstitch around the side and top edges using a ⅛" (3mm) seam allowance.

4 **Attach the hook-and-loop tape.** Sew the loop side of the hook-and-loop tape to the right side of one of the snack bag outer bag pieces. Position the tape parallel to one of the long sides, about 1" (2.5cm) from the edge, centered from side to side.

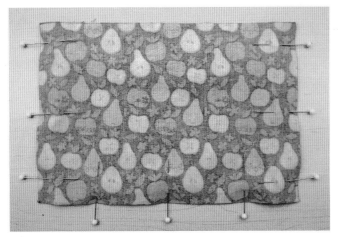

5 **Stitch the outer bag.** Place the outer bag pieces together with right sides facing and pin them in place. Using a ½" (1.5cm) seam allowance, sew around the side and bottom edges, leaving the top (with hook-and-loop tape) open. Trim the seam allowances with pinking shears and clip the corners.

6 **Baste the flap.** Turn the bag right side out. Pin the flap to the back of the outer bag with the hook-and-loop strip facing up. Align the raw bottom edge of the flap with the top edge of the bag. Baste the flap in place using a ¼" (6mm) seam allowance.

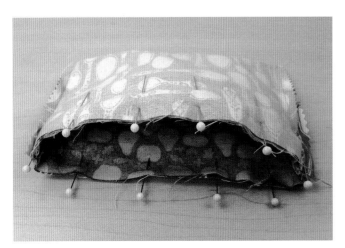

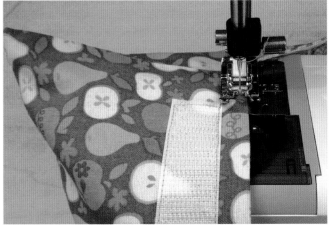

7 **Attach the lining.** Nest the outer bag inside the lining with right sides facing. Align the side seams and the raw top edges and pin the pieces in place. Stitch around the top edge of the bag using a ½" (1.5cm) seam allowance. Trim the seam allowance with pinking shears.

8 **Finish the bag.** Turn the bag right side out through the opening left in the bottom of the lining for turning. Hand stitch the opening closed using a blind stitch. Nest the lining inside the bag and press the top edge. Using a ⅛" (3mm) seam allowance, stitch around the top edge of the bag. Repeat as desired to make additional snack bags.

Shopping Cart Caddy

Materials & Tools:
- Fabric A: ⅔ yd. (0.6m) cotton or other (front)
- Fabric B: ⅔ yd. (0.6m) cotton or other (back)
- Fabric C: ⅓ yd. (0.3m) cotton or other (pockets)
- Lightweight or medium-weight, fusible interfacing: 1¼ yd. (1.1m), 45" (114.5cm) wide
- Coordinating fabric for notepad cover (optional): ¼ yd. (0.25m)
- Hook-and-loop tape: 2" (50mm) wide
- Walking foot (optional)

This shopping caddy is easy to attach to the handle of most grocery store carts. Use it to keep your shopping list, pen, and coupons organized and easily accessible during your next trip to the grocery store. This piece is also machine washable, so you can keep it clean. Make it in fabrics that coordinate with your reusable grocery totes (see page 88)! Or make a coordinating cover for your favorite shopping notepad. You can adapt this project to any situation where you might need a handy caddy organizer, like out in the garden, or for a baby stroller.

Cutting Chart

Follow the chart below to cut the pieces for this project from the total fabric yardage indicated in the Materials & Tools list above.

Piece Name	Material to Cut	Size to Cut	Quantity
Front	Fabric A	21" x 19" (53.5 x 48.5cm)	1
Back	Fabric B	21" x 19" (53.5 x 48.5cm)	1
Pockets	Fabric C	5½" x 19" (14 x 48.5cm)	2
Interfacing	Light/medium-weight, fusible	20¾" x 18¾" (52.5 x 47.5cm)	1
Pocket interfacing (optional)	Light/medium-weight, fusible	4½" x 18¾" (11.5 x 52.5cm)	2
Hook-and-loop tape		2" x 1½" (50mm x 4cm)	3

1 Prepare the pockets. If you would like to reinforce your pockets, follow the manufacturer's instructions to fuse the pocket interfacing pieces to the wrong side of the pocket pieces. Fold over the top edge of both pocket pieces and the bottom edge of the top pocket piece by ¼" (6mm). Press these folds in place. Repeat, folding the edges over again and pressing them in place. Stitch the double folds on the top edges in place using a ⅛" (3mm) seam allowance; do not stitch the folds on the bottom edge of the top pocket.

2 Mark the pocket locations. Use a disappearing marker to mark the seams that will divide the pockets. You can divide your pockets as desired. For the project shown, the top pocket piece has a 1" (2.5cm)-wide pen pocket in the center. To mark this, measure in 8½" (21.5cm) and 9½" (24cm) from one of the short ends. The bottom pocket piece was divided into three pockets of the same size. To mark this, measure in 6" (15cm) and 12" (30cm) from one of the short ends.

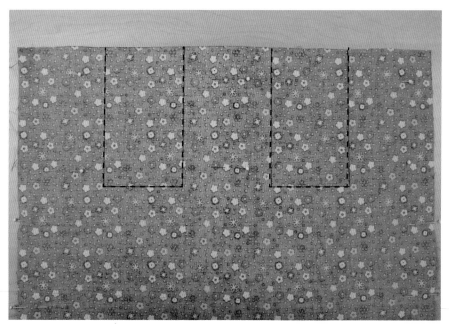

3 Prepare the body. Following the manufacturer's instructions, fuse the interfacing to the wrong side of the front piece. Pin the front and back pieces together with right sides facing. Mark rectangles along one of the 19" (48.5cm) edges. To do this, start at the left side and measure in 4" (10cm), down 6" (15cm), right 3½" (9cm), and up 6" (15cm). This completes the first rectangle. Repeat, measuring in from the right side to draw the second rectangle. Cut out the rectangles and separate the front and back pieces.

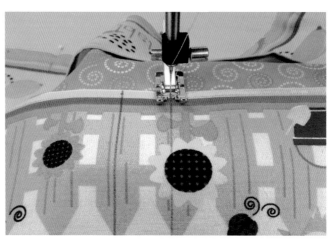

4 Position the pockets. Pin the bottom pocket to the front piece, aligning the bottom edges. Both pieces should be right side up. Pin the top pocket to the front piece, positioning it 2" (5cm) above the bottom pocket.

5 Stitch the pockets. Using a ⅛" (3mm) seam allowance, stitch along the bottom edge of the top pocket. Stitch along all the dividing lines you marked on the pocket pieces in Step 2. For each line, start at the bottom of the pocket and stitch toward the top to prevent puckering. Remember to backstitch at the top of each dividing line to make sure the seams are sturdy. Using a ¼" (6mm) seam allowance, baste the sides of both pocket pieces and the bottom edge of the bottom pocket piece to the front piece.

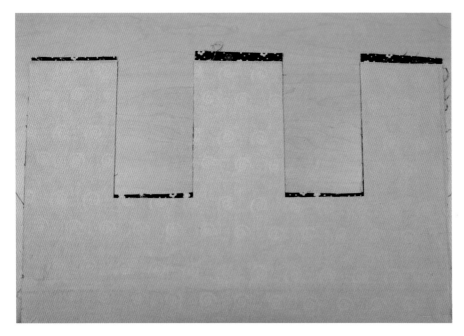

6 Pin the body. Place the front and back pieces together with right sides facing. Smooth out the fabric of both layers very well, matching up the bottom and side edges. Pin the pieces together. If there is excess backing fabric due to shrinkage of the front piece, trim it away.

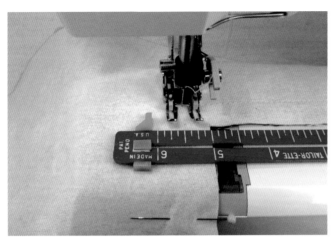

7 **Stitch the body.** Place a walking foot in your sewing machine. Using a ½" (1.5cm) seam allowance, sew around all the edges of the body, leaving a 4"–6" (10–15cm) opening in the bottom edge for turning. Use a ruler when sewing the corners around the rectangular cutouts to be sure you are maintaining the ½" (1.5cm) seam allowance.

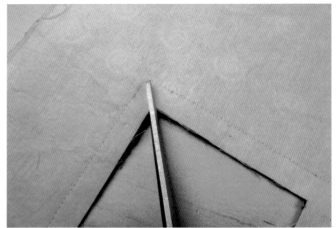

8 **Finish the caddy.** Clip the corners of the rectangular cutouts as close to the stitch line as possible and trim the seam allowances. Turn the caddy right side out through the opening left in the bottom edge for turning and press it. Hand stitch the opening closed using a blind stitch. Using a ⅛" (3mm) seam allowance, stitch around all edges of the body.

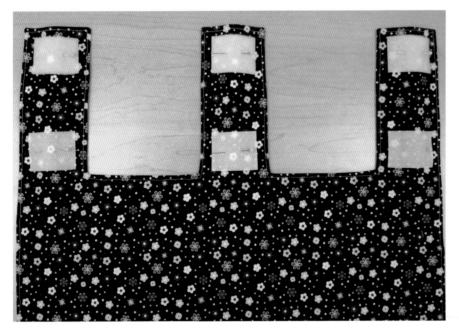

9 **Attach the hook-and-loop tape.** Attach a pair of hook-and-loop tabs to the back side of each of the straps. Center the tabs on the straps, placing the top tabs about ¼" (0.5cm) from the top edge, and the bottom tabs about ¼" (0.5cm) from the bottom edge of the rectangular cutouts. Using a thread that coordinates with the front fabric and a ⅛" (3mm) seam allowance, stitch around the edges of the tabs to secure them in place.

Stylish Grocery Tote Set

Materials & Tools:

- Fabric A: 1 yd. (1m) heavy canvas (outer bag)
- Fabric B: 1 yd. (1m) cotton or other (lining)
- Fabric C: ⅔ yd. (0.6m) cotton or other (handles)
- Fabric D: ½ yd. (0.5m) cotton or other (storage bag)
- Nylon or cotton cording
- 1 slide bead with lock
- Walking foot (optional)
- Bodkin or safety pin

Reusable grocery bags are rapidly becoming an essential, as some cities and regions are requiring consumers to bring their own bags to the store. We love the idea and have made it a habit to always have five or six of these in the trunk of the car for weekly grocery shopping. The bags featured here use a sturdy and economical canvas for the exterior, paired with a vibrant quilting fabric for the lining and straps. Make the accompanying drawstring storage bag to hold additional essentials.

Cutting Chart

Follow the chart below to cut the pieces for this project from the total fabric yardage indicated in the Materials & Tools list above.

Piece Name	Material to Cut	Size to Cut	Quantity
Outer bag (front/back)	Fabric A	13" x 36" (33 x 91.5cm)	2
Outer bag (sides)	Fabric A	8" x 15" (20.5 x 38cm)	4
Lining (front/back; cut selvage to selvage)	Fabric B	13" x 39" (33 x 99cm)	2
Lining (sides)	Fabric B	8" x 16½" (20.5 x 42cm)	4
Handles (cut on the grain)*	Fabric C	4" x 28½" (10 x 72.5cm)	8
Storage bag	Fabric D	13" x 15" (33 x 38cm)	2
Cording	Nylon or cotton	36" (90cm)	1

Remember, the grain always runs parallel to the selvages

1 Stitch the handles. Place two handle strips together with right sides facing. Pin and stitch the strips together along one of the short ends using a ½" (1.5cm) seam allowance. Repeat to attach two more handle strips to make one long strip. Sew the two loose ends of the strip together to make one giant loop approximately 110" (280cm) in circumference. Repeat with the remaining four handle strips to make a second loop.

2 Fold the handles. Press the seams open on both handle loops. Then, fold each handle loop in half lengthwise with wrong sides facing and press the fold in place. Open the handle loops and fold each long edge in until it meets the center crease. Press these folds in place. Fold the handle loops in half lengthwise along the center crease as before.

3 Mark the lining pieces. Take one of the lining body pieces and fold it in half widthwise, bringing the short ends together. Make a mark on the center crease at both ends to mark the center point. Repeat this with two of the lining side panels, but fold them in half lengthwise, bringing the long edges together.

4 Pin the lining pieces. Lay the marked lining body piece face up. Pin one of the side panel pieces onto the main body piece, matching up the center marks with right sides facing. The pieces should be perpendicular, with one of the short ends of the side piece pinned to one of the long ends of the main body piece. Repeat to pin the remaining side panel to the other long edge of the main body piece, matching up the center marks.

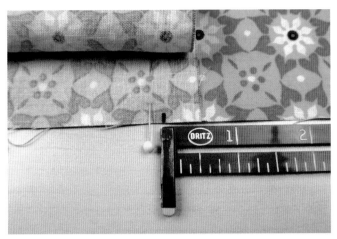

5 **Mark the side panels.** On the end of one side panel pinned to the main body piece, measure in ½" (1.5cm) from each long edge and make a mark. Repeat with the second side panel.

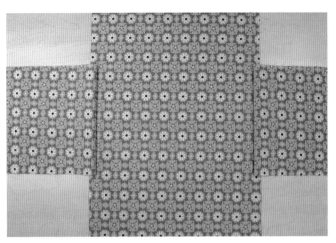

6 **Stitch the side panels.** Using a ½" (1.5cm) seam allowance, stitch the side panels to the main body piece, starting and stopping ½" (1.5cm) from each long edge where you marked in Step 5. When finished, the pieces will form a cross as shown.

7 **Clip the corners.** Lay the main body piece with the side panels attached wrong side up. Clip the edge of the main body piece where the stitching for the side panels ends. Clip in to the stitch line so the fabric can freely pivot at the corners. You will make four clips, one at each end of the stitching for both side panels.

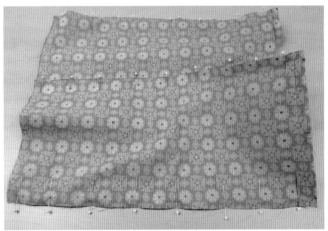

8 **Pin the side panels.** Pin the edges of the side panels to the corresponding edges of the main body piece. Start by aligning and pinning the top corners of each side piece to the corresponding corners of the main body piece with right sides facing. Then, pin the edges of the side pieces to the corresponding edges of the main body piece, working down from the top corners. When you reach the bottom corners, pivot the main body fabric where you clipped it to align the main body edge with the side piece edge.

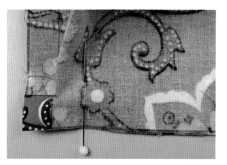

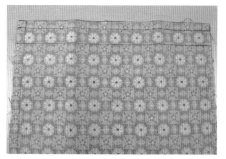

9 **Check the bottom corners.** When pinned, the bottom corners should look like this. The clip in the main body fabric allows the fabric to pivot so the edge aligns with the side panel edge. This leaves a small square of open space at the corner.

10 **Stitch the side panels.** Using a ½" (1.5cm) seam allowance, stitch along all the pinned edges to attach the edges of the side panels to the corresponding edges of the main body piece. When finished, the bottom corners should look exactly as they did when you pinned them.

11 **Mark the lining.** Lay out the stitched lining piece with wrong sides out. On the front side, mark two parallel lines along the top edge. The first should be ½" (1.5cm) down from the top edge, and the second should be 1¼" (3cm) down from the first line. Repeat on the back side.

12 **Fold the top edge.** Using the marks you made in Step 11 as a guide, fold over the top edge of the lining piece at the ½" (1.5cm) point and press the fold in place. Then fold the edge over at the 1¼" (3cm) point and press the fold in place.

13 **Mark the handle placement.** Take one of the outer bag canvas pieces and place it right side up. Draw a line parallel to each long edge of the piece, 2½" (6.5cm) from the raw edge. This marks the placement of the handles.

14 **Mark the handle loops and the canvas.** Lay both handle loops flat and mark the creases at each end as shown. Fold the marked canvas body piece in half widthwise, bringing the short ends together. Make a sharp crease at the fold. This marks the bottom center of the bag.

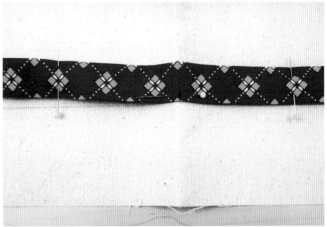

15 **Pin one side of a handle loop.** Open up the canvas piece. Take one of the handle loops and align the long edge with one of the lines marked on the canvas, matching up the center crease of the canvas with one of the marks on the handle loop. Working outward from the center point, pin the handle loop along the line marked on the canvas.

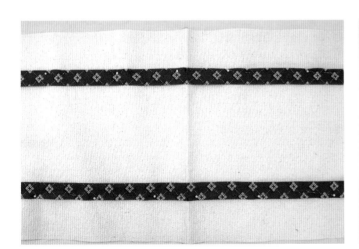

16 **Pin the other side.** Pin the other side of the handle loop in place along the other edge of the canvas piece, aligning the center point of the canvas with the remaining mark on the handle loop. Be sure there are no twists in the handle loop before pinning it in place. When finished pinning, the handle loop should look like this.

17 **Stitch the handles.** Next to each of the handle straps, make a mark 1¼" (3cm) in from the short ends of the canvas piece. Using a ⅛" (3mm) seam allowance, stitch along both long edges of the handle loop, starting and stopping 1¼" (3cm) away from the short ends of the canvas piece where you marked. Don't forget to backstitch at the beginning and end of each seam.

18 **Mark the outer bag pieces.** Repeat Step 3 with the outer bag pieces, marking the center point widthwise on the canvas piece with the handles attached, and marking the center point lengthwise on the canvas side pieces.

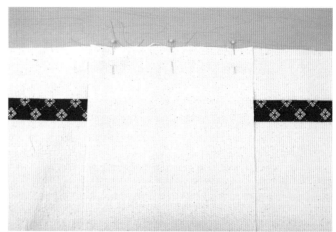

19 **Pin and stitch the outer bag pieces.** Repeat Step 4 to pin the outer bag side pieces to the outer bag main body with right sides facing, matching up the center points. Repeat Step 5 to mark the pinned ends of the side pieces. Then, repeat Step 6 to stitch the side pieces in place, stopping and starting ½" (1.5cm) from each long edge you marked.

20 **Clip the corners.** Repeat Step 7 to clip the main body piece at each end of both stitch lines for the side panels.

21 **Pin and stitch the side panels.** Repeat Step 8 with the outer bag pieces to pin the side panels to the corresponding edges of the main body piece, working down from the top corners. Refer to Step 9 to make sure the bottom corners are pinned properly. Then repeat Step 10 to stitch the side panels to the main body piece.

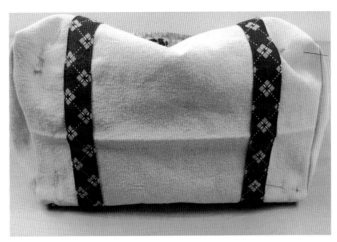

22 **Reinforce the corners.** Fold up the bottom corners and stitch across them, within the seam allowance, to reinforce them.

23 **Assemble the pieces.** Pin the loose handles to the outer bag to keep them out of the way. Nest the lining inside the outer bag with wrong sides facing. Align the bottom corners and temporarily pin them together.

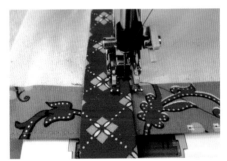

24 **Pin and stitch the top edge.** Fold the 1¼" (3cm) pressed top edge of the lining over the top edge of the outer bag so it shows on the outside of the bag. Match up all the seams and pin the top edges in place. Using a ⅛" (3mm) seam allowance, stitch around the top edge of the bag and along the bottom folded edge of the lining piece.

25 **Finish stitching the handles.** Using a ⅛" (3mm) seam allowance, stitch along the long inner edge of one handle strap, starting at the 1¼" (3cm) point where you stopped previously. When you reach the top edge of the bag, continue stitching onto the strap. Continue stitching until you reach the 1¼" (3cm) point at the other side of the handle. Repeat on the outer edge of the same handle strap. Then repeat the entire step on the remaining handle strap.

26 **Make the second bag.** Repeat with the remaining lining and outer bag pieces to create a second matching bag.

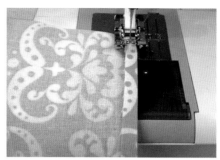

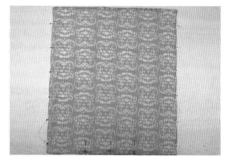

Storage Bag

1 Prepare the edges. Fold over one of the short ends of both storage bag pieces by ¼" (6mm) and press the folds in place. Using a ⅛" (3mm) seam allowance, stitch the folds in place.

2 Pin and stitch the bag body. Pin the two storage bag pieces together with right sides facing and the hemmed edges at the top. Draw a line parallel to the top (hemmed) edge, 1½" (1.5cm) down from the edge. Mark both the front and back sides of the bag. Using a ½" (1.5cm) seam allowance, stitch around the side and bottom edges of the bag, starting and stopping 1½" (4cm) from the top edge according to the mark you made.

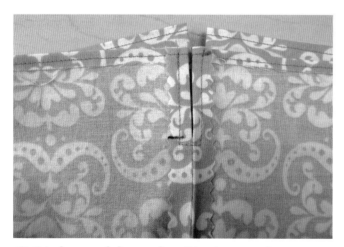

3 Stitch around the notches. Trim the seam allowances with pinking shears. Do not trim too close to the seam. Press the seams open. Using a ⅛" (3mm) seam allowance, stitch around the notches at the top of each side seam. Start at the top edge of the bag, stitch down along one side of the notch, across the bottom, and back up the other side to the top edge of the bag.

4 Fold and stitch the top edge. Fold over the top edge of the bag until it meets the 1½" (4cm) lines you marked in Step 2 and press the fold in place. Using a ⅛" (3mm) seam allowance, stitch the folds in place. You will be stitching along the ⅛" (3mm) seam you stitched in Step 1.

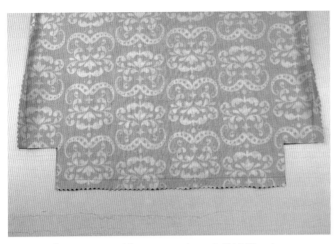

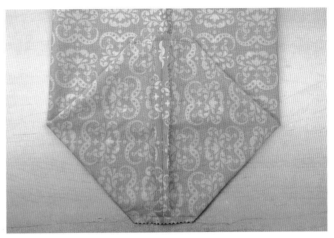

5 **Cut the corners.** Measure and mark 1¼" (3cm) squares in the bottom corners of the bag. NOTE: When measuring the squares, do not include the seam allowances; measure from the bottom and side stitch lines instead of the fabric edges. Cut out the squares.

6 **Fold and stitch the corners.** Fold the fabric so the side seams align with the bottom seam and the bottom corners form straight raw edges as shown. Pin the corners in place, and then stitch straight along the raw edges using a ½" (1.5cm) seam allowance. Trim the seam allowances with pinking shears.

7 **Add the cording.** Using a bodkin or safety pin, thread the cording through the casing at the top of the bag. Start on the right side, thread the cording all the way around the bag, and bring it out on the right side again. Thread both ends of the cording through the slide bead, and tie the ends together in a knot after the bead.

Dog Walking Pouch

- -

Materials & Tools:

- Fabric A: ¼ yd. (0.25m) cotton or other (outer bag, pockets)
- Fabric B: ⅓ yd. (0.3m) cotton or other (lining, flap, binding)
- Utility clip in your preferred size
- Hook-and-loop tape: ¾" (20mm) wide
- Walking foot (optional)
- Seam jack (optional)

- -

Here is a handy cross-body bag to use when going out for a walk with your dog. The bag is designed to hold all the essentials, from plastic waste bags and treats to your keys and phone. Hang it near your entryway so it's always ready to go!

Cutting Chart

Follow the chart below to cut the pieces for this project from the total fabric yardage indicated in the Materials & Tools list above.

Piece Name	Material to Cut	Size to Cut	Quantity
Outer bag	Fabric A	6¼" x 7¾" (16 x 19.5cm)	2
Outer front pocket	Fabric A	6¼" x 4" (16 x 10cm)	1
Outer back pocket	Fabric A	6¼" x 5½" (16 x 14cm)	1
Lining	Fabric B	6¼" x 7¾" (16 x 19.5cm)	2
Flap fabric	Fabric B	6¼" x 4" (16 x 10cm)	2
Seam binding (cut on grain)*	Fabric B	1¾" x 36" (4.5 x 91.5cm)	2
Hook-and-loop tape		¾" x 4" (20mm x 10cm)	1

Cut the seam binding pieces along the grain so they don't stretch out of shape.

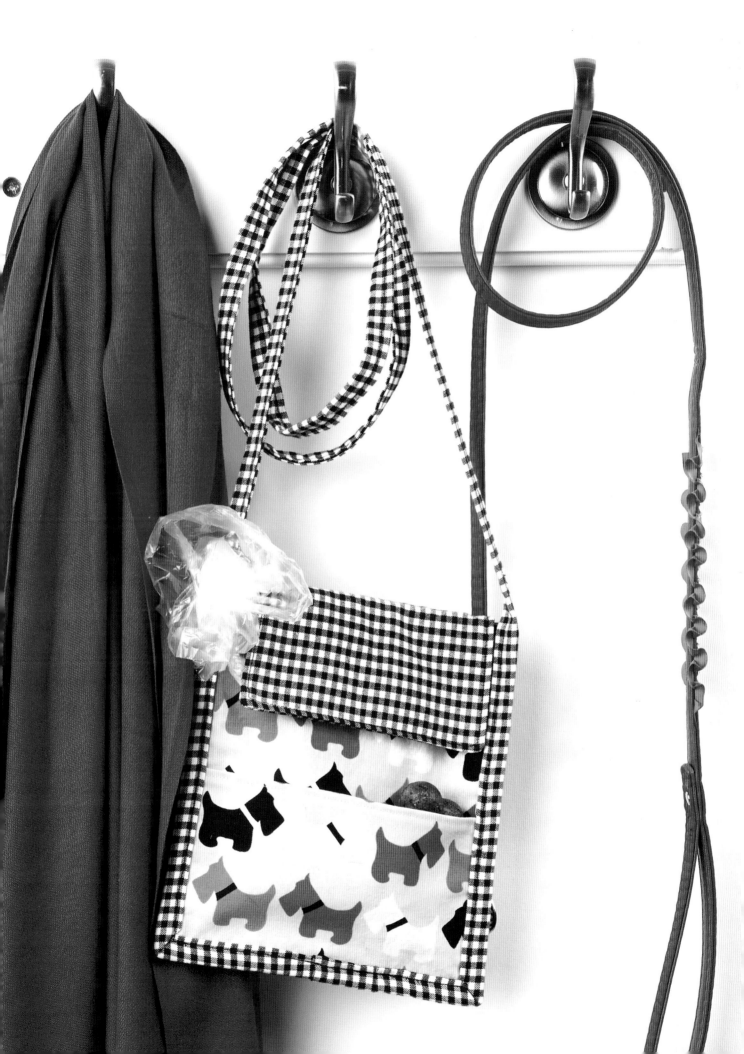

1 **Sew the binding strips.** Place the short ends of the two binding strips perpendicular to one another with right sides facing. Allow about ¼" (0.5cm) of overlap. Mark a diagonal line that extends roughly from the top corner of the top piece to the bottom corner of the bottom piece. Pin the pieces in place and stitch along this line. Trim the seam allowance with pinking shears and press it to one side.

2 **Prepare the binding.** Fold over one short end of the binding strip by ¼" (0.5cm) and press the fold in place. Then fold the strip in half lengthwise with wrong sides facing and press the fold in place. Open the strip and fold each long edge in until it meets the center crease. Press these folds in place. Fold the strip in half lengthwise along the center crease as before and press.

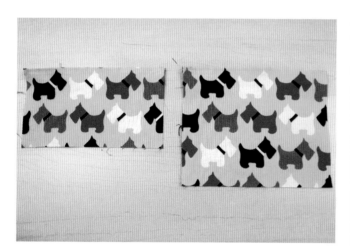

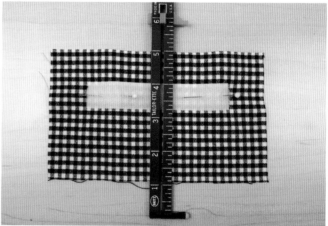

3 **Prepare the pockets.** Fold over one long edge of each pocket piece by ¼" (0.5cm). Press these folds in place. Repeat, folding the edges over again and pressing them in place. Using a ⅛" (3mm) seam allowance, topstitch the folds in place. These finished edges are the top of the pockets.

4 **Attach the hook-and-loop tape.** Take the hook side of the hook-and-loop tape and sew it to the right side of one of the flap pieces. Position the tape parallel to one of the long sides, about 1" (2.5cm) from the edge, centered from side to side.

5 **Sew the flap.** Pin the flap pieces together with right sides facing. Using a ¼" (6mm) seam allowance, stitch along the side and top edges, leaving the bottom (without hook-and-loop tape) open. Clip the corners and trim the seam allowances. Turn the flap right side out and press it, being careful not to touch the hook-and-loop tape with the iron.

6 **Finish the flap.** Using a ⅛" (3mm) seam allowance, topstitch around the side and top edges of the flap. Use the pin pull trick (see page 116) on the corners if necessary.

7 **Attach the hook-and-loop tape.** Take the loop side of the hook-and-loop tape and sew it to the right side of one of the outer bag pieces. Position the tape parallel to one of the short sides, about 2" (5cm) from the edge, centered from side to side. This piece is the front of the bag.

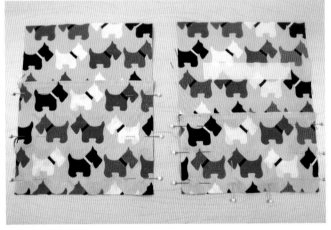

8 **Position the pockets.** Pin the short pocket to the front outer bag piece, aligning the bottom edges. Both pieces should be right side up. In the same manner, pin the tall pocket to the right side of the back outer bag piece. Using a ¼" (6mm) seam allowance, baste the sides of both pockets to their respective outer bag pieces.

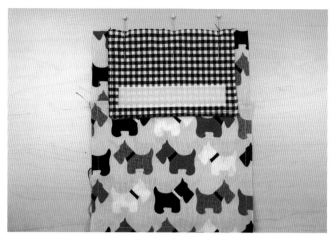

9 **Baste the flap.** Pin the flap to the outer bag back, aligning the raw bottom edge of the flap with the top edge of the bag back. Pin the pieces together with right sides facing (hook-and-loop tape out), centering the flap. Baste the flap in place using a ¼" (6mm) seam allowance.

10 **Attach the lining.** Place one of the lining pieces and the outer bag back piece together with right sides facing. Pin the pieces together along the top edge. Using a ¼" (6mm) seam allowance, stitch along the top edge only.

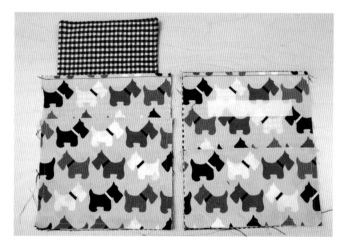

11 **Finish the top edge.** Flip the lining piece up and over the top edge of the outer bag back piece so the flap is at the top and the wrong sides of the pieces are facing. Press the top edge, and then stitch along it using a ⅛" (3mm) seam allowance. Repeat Steps 10 and 11 with the outer bag front piece and remaining lining piece.

12 **Pin the bag.** Place the two bag pieces together with wrong sides facing and pin them in place. Keep the pins away from the edges and make sure the flap is up out of the way.

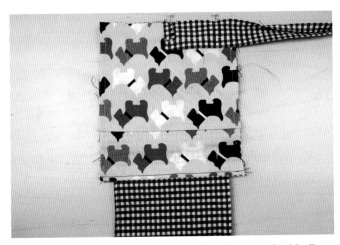

13 **Pin the binding.** Slide the utility clip onto the binding strip, pushing it toward the center out of the way. Place the bag with the back side up and the flap closest to you. Open the folds of the binding strip. Place the short folded end at the center point along the bottom of the bag. Align the long edge of the binding strip with the bottom edge of the bag with right sides facing. Pin the strip in place.

14 **Stitch to the corner.** Using a ¼" (6mm) seam allowance, stitch along the bottom edge of the bag to sew the binding strip in place. Stop ¼" (6mm) before you reach the corner of the bag. With the needle in a down position, lift the presser foot and pivot the fabric until the needle is facing the corner of the bag. Lower the presser foot and sew straight out to the tip of the corner.

15 **Fold the binding.** Backstitch at the corner, cut the threads, and remove the bag from the sewing machine. Fold the binding strip at the stitch line, folding it back toward the bottom of the bag (shown). Then fold the binding strip back on itself toward the top of the bag, aligning the fold with the bottom of the bag and the long edge with the side edge of the bag.

16 **Pin the binding.** Pin the binding in place along the side edge of the bag. Mark the diagonal fold at the corner with a disappearing marker, or run your fingernail along it several times so you can see it.

17 **Stitch to the top corner.** Resume sewing the binding by lowering the needle onto the fabric, ¼" (6mm) from the side edge, just past the diagonal fold. Backstitch (make sure you don't backstitch over the fold), and sew along the side of the bag to attach the binding. When you reach the top edge of the bag, finish off your seam and remove the bag from the machine.

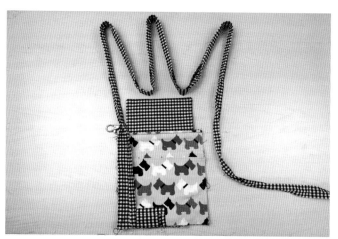

18 **Measure the strap.** Starting from the top edge of the bag where you just finished sewing, measure 50" (127cm) along the binding strip. This will be the strap. Place a pin at the 50" (127cm) mark.

19 **Pin and stitch the binding.** Starting at the 50" (127cm) mark, pin the binding along the other side of the bag. Make sure there are no twists in the strap before pinning the binding in place. Using a ¼" (6mm) seam allowance, stitch along the edge of the binding, stopping ¼" (6mm) from the bottom corner of the bag.

20 **Finish the corner.** Repeat Step 14 to pivot the bag and stitch out to the bottom corner. Repeat Step 15 to fold the binding back along the diagonal stitch line and then fold it back over itself, aligning the edge with the bottom of the bag.

21 **Stitch the binding.** Repeat Step 16 to pin the binding in place along the bottom of the bag and mark the corner fold. Using a ¼" (6mm) seam allowance, stitch along the bottom edge of the bag toward your starting point. Overlap the starting end of the binding strip by 1" (2.5cm) with the finishing end of the binding strip. Trim away any excess.

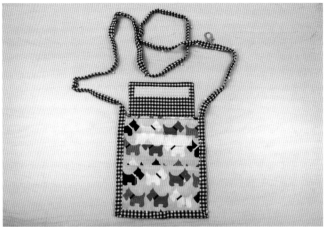

22 **Fold over the binding.** Turn the bag so the front side is facing up. Go to the starting end of the binding strip and fold it over the bottom edge of the bag onto the front side and pin it in place. Use the creases in the binding as a guide. Continue folding the binding onto the front of the bag. When you reach the strap, pin the folds in place along the strap. Then fold over and pin the binding in place along the remaining side and bottom edge of the bag.

23 **Topstitch the binding.** Starting at the bottom edge of the bag where the two ends of the binding come together, topstitch along the edge of the binding using a ⅛" (3mm) seam allowance. Use the pin pull trick (see page 116) on the corners if needed. A seam jack can also be useful for sewing the corners.

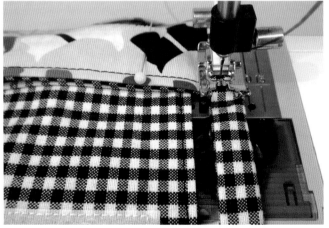

24 **Stitch the strap.** When you reach the top edge of the bag, continue stitching onto the strap to sew the long open edge closed. Keep pushing the utility clip ahead of your needle until you reach the other end of the strap. Backstitch, cut your threads, and push the utility clip back up the strap where you've already stitched. Then resume topstitching where you left off. Stitch onto the bag, along the remaining side and bottom edge until you reach your starting point.

Pampered Pooch Dog Carrier

Materials & Tools:

- Fabric A: ½ yd. (0.5m) cotton or other (outer bag sides)
- Fabric B: ⅔ yd. (0.6m) cotton or other (outer bag front/back, outer bag bottom)
- Fabric C: ¾ yd. (0.7m) cotton or other (lining, slipcover)
- Mesh fabric: 8" x 7" (20.5 x 18cm)
- Heavyweight or craft weight interfacing: 1½ yd. (1.5m), 17" (43cm) wide
- 1 package of extra-wide, double-fold bias tape in a coordinating color
- Sturdy base (foam core, plastic, wood veneer, etc.): 7¾" x 15¾" (19.5 x 40cm)
- Circle template: 4½" (11.5cm) diameter
- Hook-and-loop tape: ¾" (20mm) wide
- Pom-pom trim: 1 yd. (1m)

This dog carrier is designed to hold an adorable pet that weighs up to seven pounds. This bag features some unique fabric combinations so you and your best friend are sure to look super stylish. There's enough room for your pet to stand and look through the mesh window or curl up for a nap. For extra comfort and warmth, add a matching interior pillow or little blanket.

Cutting Chart

Follow the chart below to cut the pieces for this project from the total fabric yardage indicated in the Materials & Tools list above. Note that the front panel uses two layers of interfacing, one on the outer fabric and one on the lining fabric.

Piece Name	Material to Cut	Size to Cut	Quantity
Outer bag (sides)	Fabric A	17" x 13" (43 x 33cm)	2
Outer bag (front)	Fabric B	9" x 8" (23 x 20.5cm)	1
Outer bag (back)	Fabric B	9" x 13" (23 x 33cm)	1
Outer bag (bottom)	Fabric B	9" x 17" (23 x 43cm)	1
Handles	Fabric B	6" x 26" (15 x 66cm)	2
Lining (sides)	Fabric C	17" x 13" (43 x 33cm)	2
Lining (front)	Fabric C	9" x 8" (23 x 20cm)	1
Lining (back)	Fabric C	9" x 13" (23 x 33cm)	1
Lining (bottom)	Fabric C	9" x 17" (23 x 43cm)	1
Lining (slipcover)	Fabric C	9¼" x 17" (23.5 x 43cm)	1
Lining (slipcover)	Fabric C	9¼" x 19" (23.5 x 48.5cm)	1
Interfacing (sides)	Heavy/craft weight	16¾" x 12¾" (42.5 x 32.5cm)	2
Interfacing (front)	Heavy/craft weight	8¾" x 7¾" (22 x 19.5cm)	2
Interfacing (back)	Heavy/craft weight	8¾" x 12¾" (22 x 32.5cm)	1
Interfacing (bottom)	Heavy/craft weight	8¾" x 16¾" (22 x 42.5cm)	1
Mesh fabric	Utility weight	8" x 7" (20.5 x 18cm)	1
Hook-and-loop tape		¾" x 8" (20mm x 20cm)	1

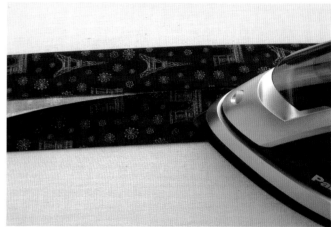

1 **Trim the corners.** Place the two outer bag side pieces together with right sides facing. Position the pieces with one of the long edges at the top. Measure and make a mark along the top edge of the fabric that is 4" (10cm) in from the left edge. Measure and make a mark along the left edge of the fabric that is 5" (12.5cm) down from the top edge. Draw a diagonal line connecting these marks, and then cut along this line. Repeat with the lining and interfacing side pieces.

2 **Prepare the handles.** Fold each handle piece in half lengthwise with wrong sides facing and press the fold in place. Open each handle piece and fold each long edge in until it meets the center crease. Press these folds in place. Fold each handle in half lengthwise along the center crease as before. Stitch along the long open edge using a ⅛" (3mm) seam allowance. Leave the short ends raw.

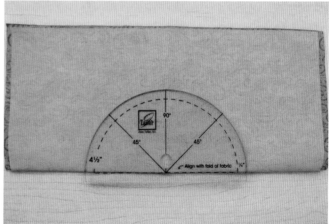

3 **Apply interfacing and mark the center point.** Following the manufacturer's instructions, fuse an interfacing front piece to the wrong side of the lining front piece. Fold the front piece in half lengthwise, and then in half widthwise with right sides facing to find the center point. Mark the center point.

4 **Mark and cut the circle.** Unfold the front piece once so that it is only folded in half. Fold your circle template in half if necessary and align the folded edge with the folded edge of the fabric. Place the center point of the circle template over the point marked on the fabric. Trace the half circle onto the fabric, and then cut it out.

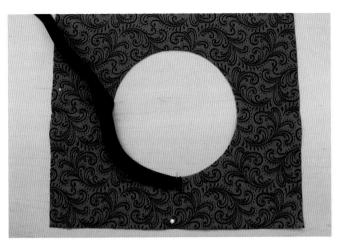

5 **Begin stitching the bias tape.** Unfold the lining front piece and place it right side up. Starting at the bottom of the circle, fold the end of the bias tape over the edge of the circular cut. Working clockwise, continue to fold the bias tape around the circular cut for several inches. Then stitch the folded tape in place, stitching ¹⁄₁₆" (2mm) from the edge of the tape.

6 **Finish stitching the bias tape.** Continue folding and stitching the bias tape until you are about 4" (10cm) from the starting end. Cut the loose end of the bias tape so it is long enough to overlap the starting end by 1" (2.5cm). Open up the manufacturer's folds in the loose end of the bias tape. Fold the short end under by ½" (1.5cm) and then refold the tape. Then continue to fold and stitch the tape around the circular cut until you reach the end of the tape.

7 **Attach the first side panel.** Pin one long edge of the lining bottom piece to one long edge of a lining side piece with right sides facing. Make a mark along the pinned edge ½" (1.5cm) in from each end. Sew the pieces together using a ½" (1.5cm) seam allowance, starting and stopping ½" (1.5cm) from each end following the markings.

8 **Attach the second side panel.** Repeat Step 7 to attach the remaining lining side piece to the other side of the lining bottom piece. When stitching the pieces together, leave an 8" (20.5cm) opening for turning. Remember to backstitch on both sides of the opening for turning. Make sure the cut corners of the side pieces are on the front end of the bottom piece. Press the seams outward.

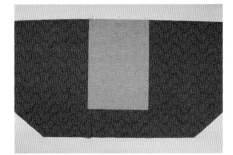

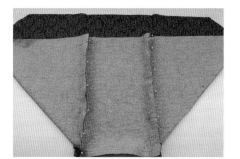

9 **Pin the back panel.** When finished with Step 8, the lining side pieces will be attached to the lining bottom piece. The cut corners of the lining side pieces will be at the front end of the bottom piece. Pin one of the short ends of the lining back piece to the back end of the bottom piece with right sides facing.

10 **Stitch the back panel.** Place pins in the back piece to mark the seam lines where the bottom panel meets the side panels (this will be about ½" [1.5cm] from each long side of the back piece). Using a ½" (1.5cm) seam allowance, stitch from end pin to end pin to attach the back piece to the bottom panel.

11 **Pin and stitch the back panel sides.** Pin the edges of the back piece to the corresponding edges of the side panels. Start by aligning and pinning the top corners of the back piece to the corresponding corners of the side panels with right sides facing. Then, pin the edges of the back piece to the corresponding edges of the side panels, working down from the top corners. Using a ½" (1.5cm) seam allowance, stitch along the pinned edges to attach the back panel to the side pieces.

12 **Attach the front piece.** Attach the front piece to the lining in the same way you attached the back piece. When stitching the edges together, stop ½" (1.5cm) from the top corners of the front piece.

13 **Create the outer front piece.** Following the manufacturer's instructions, apply all the interfacing pieces to the wrong side of their corresponding outer bag pieces. Repeat Steps 3–6 to make an outer bag front piece that matches the lining front piece.

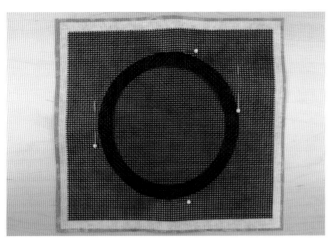

14 **Prepare the mesh fabric.** Using a rotary cutter and mat, cut the mesh fabric to 1" (2.5cm) smaller than the outer bag front piece on all sides. Pin the mesh to the back side of the front piece.

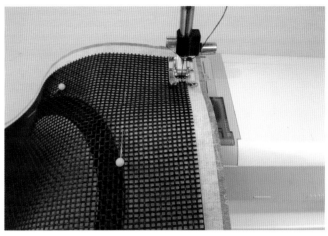

15 **Stitch the mesh fabric.** Using a ⅛" (3mm) seam allowance and a thread that coordinates with the outer bag fabric, stitch around all four sides of the mesh fabric to attach it to the front piece. You can also sew around the circular cutout again for extra strength if desired.

16 **Assemble the outer bag.** Repeat the same basic procedure used to assemble the bag lining to assemble the outer bag. Stitch the long edges of the side panels to the sides of the bottom piece. Stitch one short end of the back piece to the back end of the bottom piece. Stitch one short end of the front piece to the front end of the bottom piece. Do not sew the front and back pieces to the side panels yet.

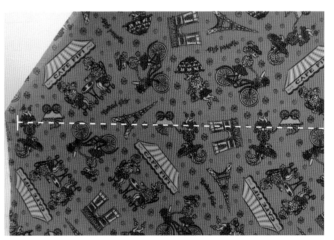

17 **Mark the trim placement.** If you wish to add trim around the outside of the bag, now is the best time to mark its placement. Draw a line across the side and back pieces, parallel to the top and bottom edges, 7" (18cm) up from the bottom seam. On both side pieces, measure in ½" (1.5cm) from the front end. Mark this on top of the line you drew for the trim. This is where you will start sewing the trim.

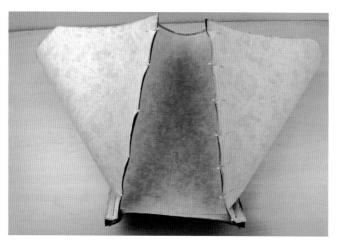

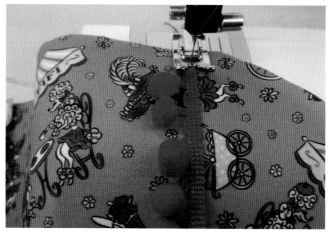

18 **Pin and stitch the back panel edges.** Repeat Step 11 to pin and stitch the outer bag back panel to the side panels. Wait to stitch the front panel to the side panels until the trim has been added. Trim the seam allowances of all the sewn seams with pinking shears.

19 **Attach the trim.** Align the top of the trim with the marks you drew in Step 17. Place the starting end of the trim on one of the side pieces, ½" (1.5cm) from the front end where you marked. Stitch the trim to the side piece. Continue stitching the trim in place around the back and onto the other side. Stop stitching ½" (1.5cm) from the front end on the other side of the bag where you marked.

20 **Pin and stitch the front panel sides.** Repeat Step 12 to pin and stitch the outer bag front panel to the side panels. Remember to stop stitching ½" (1.5cm) from the top corners of the front panel. Trim any un-trimmed seam allowances with pinking shears and turn the outer bag right side out.

21 **Mark the handle placement.** Mark the placement of the handles on the top edge of both sides of the outer bag. Make marks ½" (1.5cm) from the front end and 4½" (11.5cm) from the back end.

22 **Baste the handles.** Pin the handle ends to the outer bag, aligning the short ends of the handles with the top edge of the bag and placing the sides of the handles just inside the marks you made in Step 21. Make sure the handles are not twisted. Baste the ends in place using a ¼" (6mm) seam allowance.

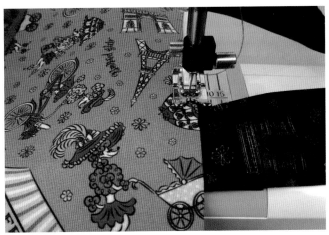

23 **Attach the lining.** Nest the outer bag inside the lining with right sides facing. Carefully align the corner seams and the raw top edges and pin the pieces in place. Starting at the front end of one side panel, stitch around the top edge to the same point on the other side using a ½" (1.5cm) seam allowance. Trim the seam allowance with pinking shears. Then stitch across the top edge of the front panel. Do not trim away the seam allowance.

24 **Finish the bag.** Turn the bag right side out through the opening left in the bottom of the lining for turning. Hand stitch the opening closed using a blind stitch. Nest the lining inside the bag and press the top edge. Using a ⅛" (3mm) seam allowance, stitch around the top edge of the bag.

Slipcover

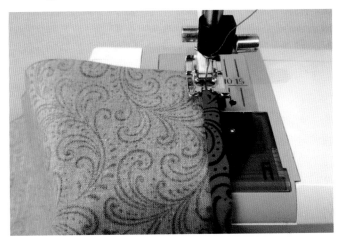

1 **Hem the edge.** Fold over one of the short ends of the 9¼" x 17" (23.5 x 43cm) slipcover piece by ¼" (0.5cm). Press the fold in place. Repeat, folding the edge over again and pressing it in place. Stitch the double fold in place using a ⅛" (3mm) seam allowance.

2 **Attach the hook-and-loop tape.** Sew the hook side of the hook-and-loop tape strip to the right side of the hemmed slipcover piece. Position the tape parallel to the hemmed side, about ½" (1.5cm) from the edge, centered from side to side.

3 **Pin the slipcover pieces.** Pin the two slipcover pieces together with right sides facing . The extra length of the longer piece should be at the same end as the hook-and-loop strip on the shorter piece. The extra length will form the flap.

4 **Stitch the slipcover.** Using a ½" (1.5cm) seam allowance, sew around the side and bottom edges of the slipcover pieces, leaving the top (flap end) open. Trim the seam allowances with pinking shears. Also trim around all sides of the flap.

5 **Finish the flap.** Turn the slipcover right side out. Fold over the three edges of the flap by ¼" (0.5cm), clipping the corners as necessary. Stitch the folds in place using a ⅛" (3mm) seam allowance. Sew the loop side of the hook-and-loop tape strip onto the flap, parallel to the top side, ½" (1.5cm) from the edge, and centered side to side.

6 **Finish the base.** Slide your sturdy base into your slipcover and place it in the bottom of your dog carrier.

Tip

In addition to the base, you can make a coordinating cushion for the bottom of the carrier. Don't forget a matching blanket!

Tools and Techniques

The projects in this book were made using the following tools. Check to make sure you have these items available before you get started.

- Steam iron
- Seam gauge
- Straight pins
- Scissors
- Pinking shears
- Rotary cutter
- Rotary cutting mat
- Clear quilting ruler
- Circle templates
- Needle and thread for handwork
- Disappearing marker
- Fabric glue

Techniques and Accessories

The following techniques and accessories are useful for sewing these projects.

Seam allowances

Use ½" (1.5cm) seam allowances for all projects unless directed otherwise.

Pin pull trick

The pin pull trick is handy for turning corners when sewing very close to the edge of the fabric, such as when topstitching using a ⅛" (3mm) seam allowance.

Begin sewing the seam on a straight edge. When you come to the corner, stop, lift the presser foot, and pivot the fabric into place to sew around the corner. Before lowering the presser foot, stick a straight pin into the corner of the fabric from the right side just behind the needle. Lower the presser foot and begin sewing, using the pin like a handle to gently pull the fabric through the machine so that the corner fabric does not bunch up under the presser foot.

Seam jack

A seam jack is an accessory that raises the height of the presser foot when sewing over a bulky area or seam. Placed under the back of the presser foot, it prevents the presser foot from tilting, so the fabric makes better contact with the feed dogs below.

Walking foot

A walking foot is a sewing machine attachment that has its own set of feed dogs to help move the fabric through the sewing machine. It is most useful when sewing heavy fabrics or sewing through many layers to keep them from shifting.

Seam jack.

Use the pin pull trick for turning corners when stitching close to the edge of the fabric.

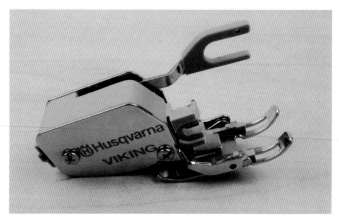

Walking foot.

Monogram Backpack: Appliqué & Embroidery (Shown at 100%)

Felt circle: 6½" (16.5cm) diameter
Fabric circle: 6" (15.5cm) diameter

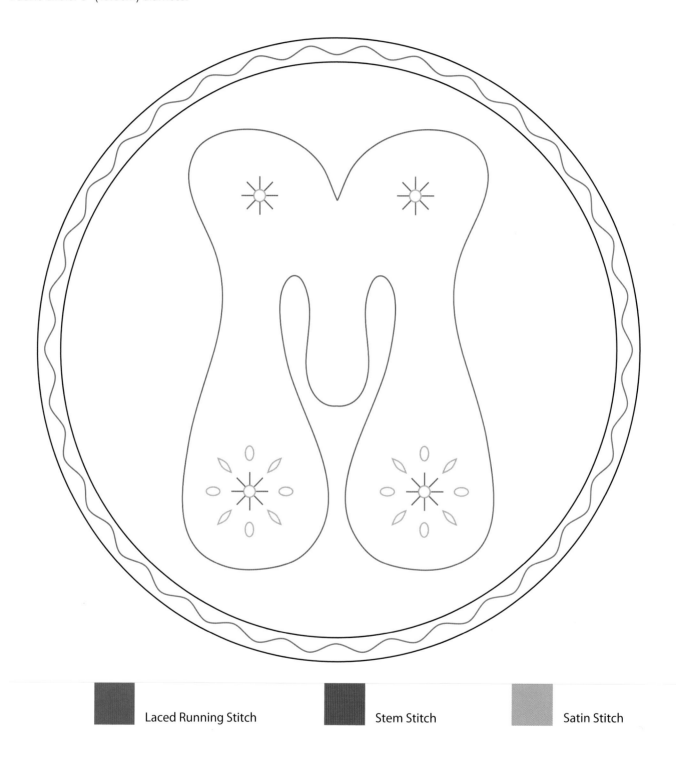

■ Laced Running Stitch   ■ Stem Stitch   ■ Satin Stitch

Patterns A–D (Shown at 100%)

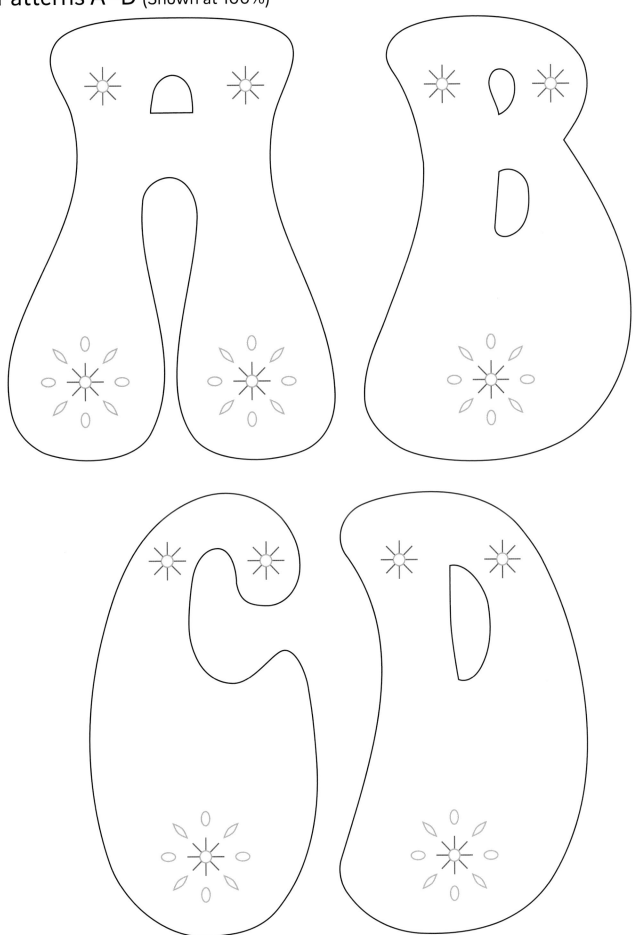

Patterns E–H (Shown at 100%)

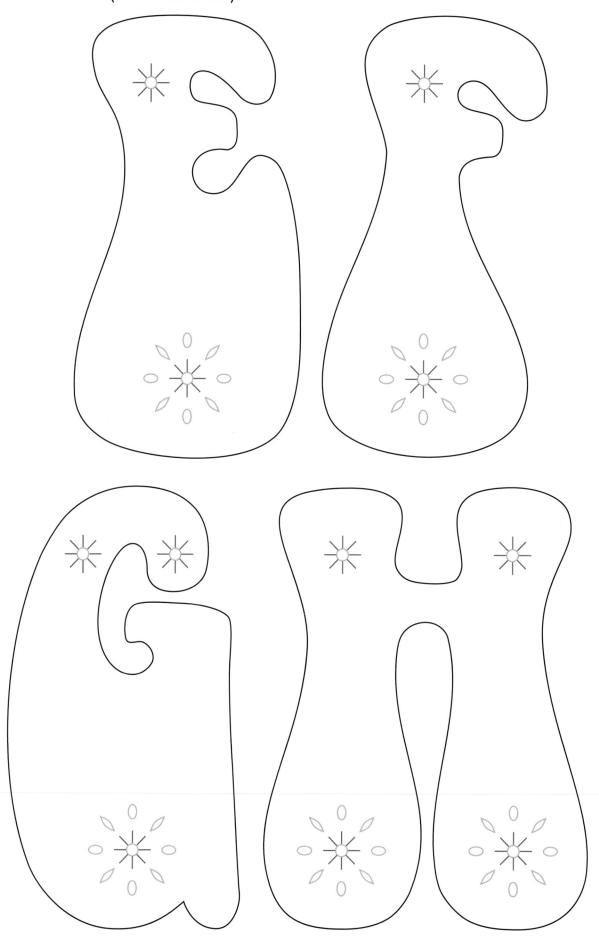

Patterns I–L (Shown at 100%)

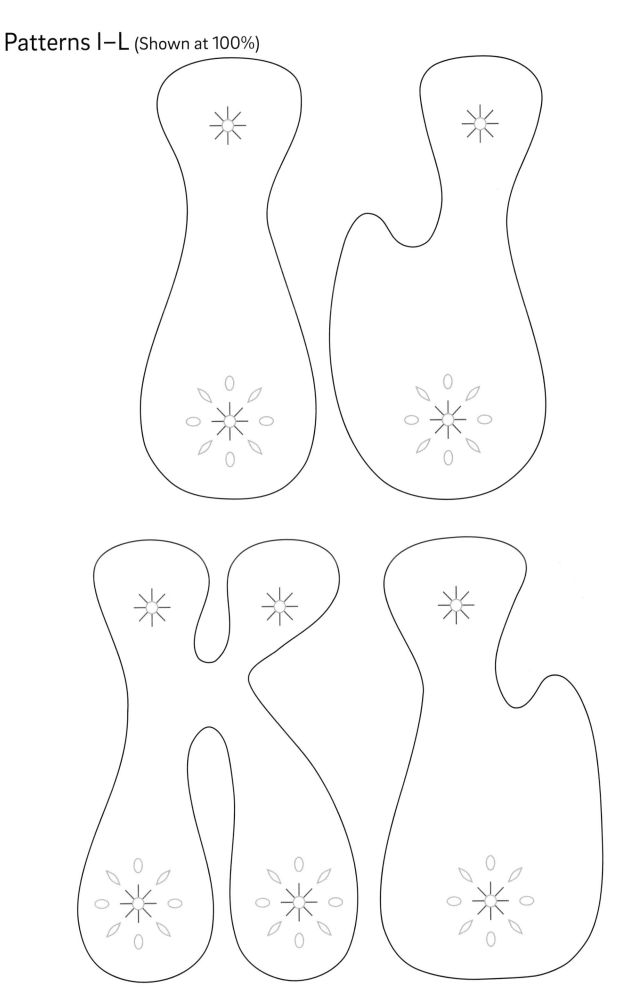

Patterns M–P (Shown at 100%)

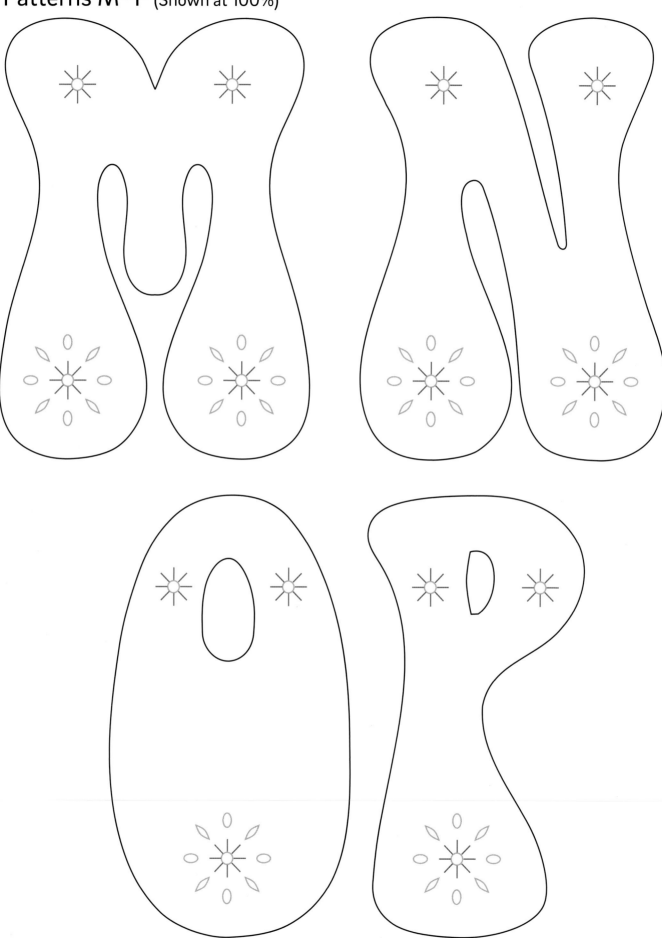

Patterns Q–U
(Shown at 100%)

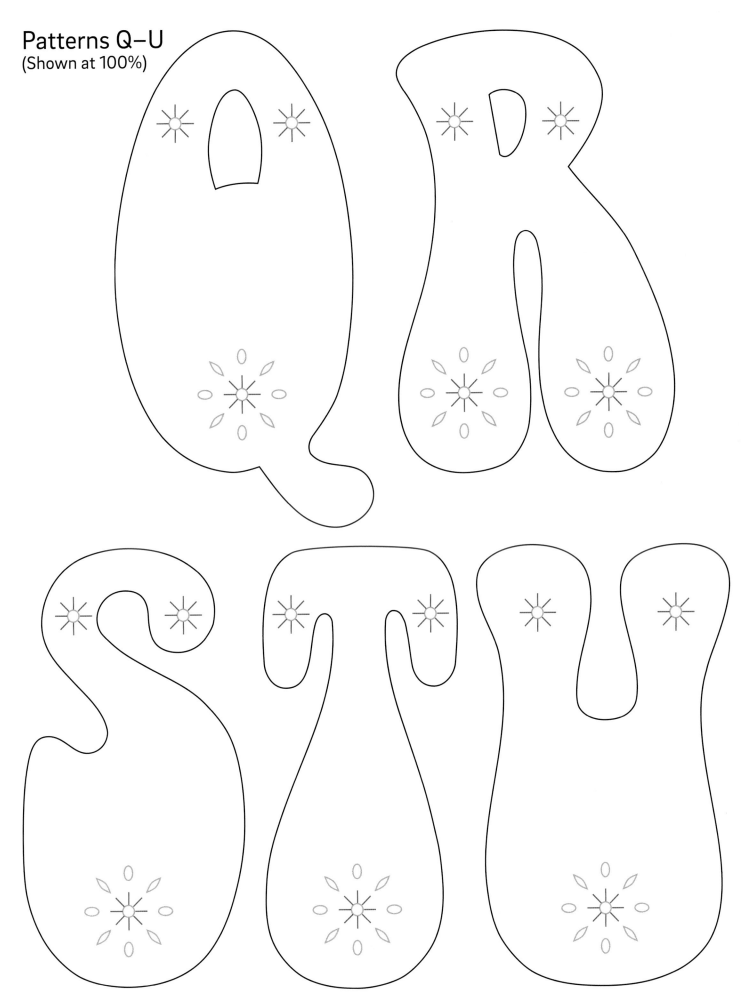

Patterns V–Z (Shown at 100%)

Boho Bag

The outer bag and lining pieces can easily be cut from a piece of fabric using a disappearing marker and a 14" (35.5cm)-diameter circle template.

1. Take one of the lining pieces and fold it in half lengthwise with right sides together so it measures 9" x 32" (23 x 81cm). Position the folded edge of the fabric on the left and the open raw edge on the right.

2. Measure 16" (40.5cm) from the bottom edge of the fabric. Use a disappearing marker to draw a line across the fabric at the 16" (40.5cm) point, parallel to the bottom edge, from folded edge to open edge.

3. Along the top edge of the fabric, measure in 2" (5cm) from the folded edge. Use a disappearing marker to draw a line down the fabric at the 2" (5cm) point. The line should be parallel to the folded edge and should run from the top edge to the 16" (40.5cm) line marked in Step 2.

4. Center the circle template over the right raw edge of the fabric. Align the bottom of the circle with the 16" (40.5cm) line and the left side of the circle with the 2" (5cm) line.

5. Trace along the bottom left quarter of the circle, from the point where the circle touches the 2" (5cm) line to the point where the circle touches the 16" (40.5cm) line.

6. Following the lines marked on the fabric, cut out the top right portion of the fabric (area to be cut away shown in pink). Start at the 16" (40.5cm) point on the right side. Cut along the curve marked by the circle template, and then continue cutting along the 2" (5cm) line to the top edge.

7. Repeat Steps 1–6 with the remaining lining piece and the outer bag front/back pieces.

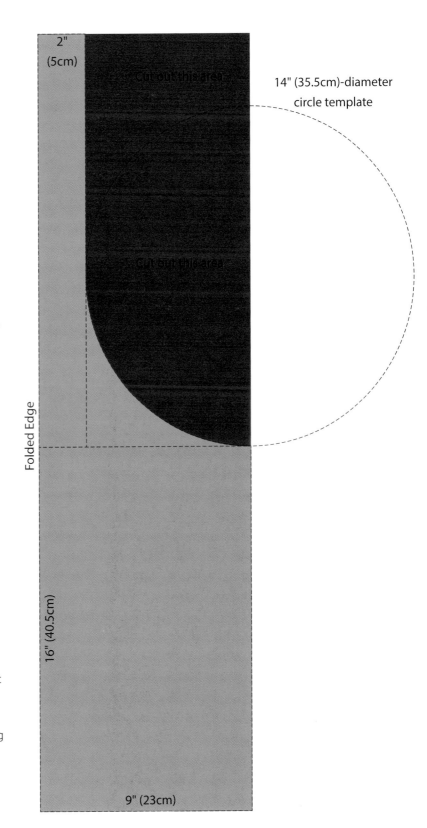

2" (5cm)

Cut out this area

Cut out this area

14" (35.5cm)-diameter circle template

Folded Edge

16" (40.5cm)

9" (23cm)

Embroidery Patterns: Boho Bag & Lunch Bag (Shown at 100%)

Stem Stitch

Double Laced Running Stitch

French Knot

Chain Stitch

Eyelet Stitch

Appliqué Fabric

Laced Running Stitch

Stem Stitch

Seed Stitch

Index

Note: Page numbers in *italics* indicate projects.

Acknowledgments

Special thanks to the professional and friendly staff at Fox Chapel Publishing in East Petersburg, Pennsylvania, for their guidance through our first book and their positive encouragement and continuous support.

Thank you to the numerous designers and textile manufacturers who generously contributed fabrics for our sewing book. The following fabrics/tools were used with the projects listed below; visit your local craft, fabric, or quilt shop to find a fabric you love: Gingham/Cherries by In-House Classic (Retro Ruffles Purse), Bloom & Berries by Teresa Woo-Murray (Stylish Grocery Tote Set), and Urban Zoologie by Ann Kelle (Dog Walking Pouch) manufactured by Robert Kaufman; Caravan Dreams by Josephine Kimberling (Mod Monogram Backpack) and Clementine by Ana Davis (Going Green Reusable Lunch Bag Set) manufactured by Blend Fabrics; and French Poodles by Pampered Girls (Pampered Pooch Dog Carrier) manufactured by Spoonflower; circle templates and rotary cutting mats by June Tailor; nonwoven fusible interfacing and cotton quilt batting by Bosal Foam & Fiber. All other fabrics by Debra Valencia through David Textiles, Inc., Wilmington Prints, and Spoonflower.

An extra big thank-you to Joanne Fink, my art licensing coach, for helping me launch my brand, always believing in me with such enthusiasm, being a dear friend, and especially for the introduction to Peg Couch, acquisition editor at Fox Chapel Publishing.

Biggest thanks possible in the world to my sister Cheyanne for doing all the sewing for the book and spending an extra four months and countless hours at my house in California so we could collaborate in person on all the project concepts, designs, instructions, prototypes, pattern making, and shopping for notions. We had a lot of fun, too, especially singing—one of our other favorite things to do together!